Sex Advice From . . .

If an expert says it can't be done, get another expert.

—David Ben-Gurion

Sex Advice From...

DJs, Sorority Girls, Cowboys, Car Dealers,
Bartenders, Pool Cleaners, Hairstylists, and More!

From the Editors of Nerve.com

CHRONICLE BOOKS
SAN FRANCISCO

Library of Congress Cataloging-in-Publication Data:

Sex advice from—DJs, sorority girls, cowboys, car dealers, bartenders, pool cleaners, haistylists, and more! / from the editors of Nerve.com.
p. cm.

ISBN-10: 0-8118-5002-1
ISBN-13: 978-0-8118-5002-5

1. Sex—Miscellanea. 2. Sex customs—Miscellanea.
3. Sex instruction—Miscellanea. I. Nerve.com (Computer file)

HQ23.S46 2006
306.77—dc22
2005029773

Manufactured in Canada

Designed by Efrat Rafaeli

Typeset by Joanne Lee

Distributed in Canada by Raincoast Books
9050 Shaughnessy Street
Vancouver, British Columbia V6P 6E5

10 9 8 7 6 5 4 3 2 1

Chronicle Books LLC
85 Second Street
San Francisco, California 94105
www.chroniclebooks.com

CONTENTS

Sex Advice From . . .

Introduction

Truth be told, when we launched the "Sex Advice from . . ." column on Nerve.com, we were looking for humorously bad sex advice. We thought that if we asked random people who happened to be life-guards or sushi chefs questions like "What's a no-fail cunnilingus technique?" they would say things like "I just love eatin' it and I never stop. There ain't no way you can't do it good." And, indeed, we did get some humorously bad sex advice (the comment above, for instance, was from a fifty-nine-year-old cowboy). But much to our surprise, most of the advice we got from citizens—each represen-tative of a specific walk of life—was humorously good. For instance, when we asked Tom, the aforementioned cowboy, to provide us with some general words of sexual wisdom, he said, "Patience. Boy, I tell you, you know what they say about it being a virtue? Well, it's true."

Then there was Aimee, a thirty-year-old publicist who, when asked what we could do to drum up good publicity to impress our latest crush, suggested launching "a good word-of-mouth . . . word-of-mouth-skills campaign." Genius! When we asked Rob, a twenty-nine-year-old model, what a guy who loses his erection during sex can do to alleviate the tension and regain momentum, he said, "Tell her it's the medication you're taking. Otherwise she'll never believe she's not fat, ugly, or old." Dan Savage couldn't have said it better.

Of course, many of the answers varied widely. If you've had sex with even one person, then you know that when it comes to preferences and proclivities everyone is unique. For example, when asked how long sex should last, Mikey, a twenty-seven-year-old record store clerk said, "An hour. . . . I've found that it's better to savor the act as a whole instead of fixating upon the release." Meanwhile, Ryan, Mikey's twenty-five-year-old colleague, told us that "the optimum is between five and ten minutes." They may aim for different durations, and recommend different tips on how to go down on a woman (Mikey was all for the good old-fashioned "writing the letters of the alphabet with the tip of the tongue" technique; Ryan recommended watching porn), but their comical, often capricious advice was surprisingly useful.

We traveled far and wide in our search for novel advice. We spoke to tour guides in Seattle; cowboys working in the California hills; used-car dealers in Dallas–Fort Worth; lifeguards in New Jersey; construction workers on Martha's Vineyard; tattoo artists in New York; pool cleaners in Hollywood; sideshow performers at Coney Island; and American expats living all over the globe.

Before sending our brave correspondents into the trenches, we spent weeks locked inside the Nerve war room, delving into memories of our own sexual mishaps and misadventures, and wracking our brains to come up with a comprehensive list of questions about all things sex—from dirty talk to home movies, hygiene, grooming, foreplay, blow jobs, tricky positions, fuck buddies, mismatched libidos, optimal sex toys, role-play, oral play, anal techniques, threesomes, orgies, and polyamorous affairs. It's everything you ever wanted to know about sex but were too afraid to ask the checkout guy at your local costume shop.

We then presented our "sexperts" with Nerve-generated questions ("My boyfriend 'finishes' too fast in bed. What can I do to help him slow things down?" "What are some do's and don'ts for making an X-rated home movie?" "What are some great anal sex tips?"), readers' questions ("Can you give me a no-fail role-playing scenario?" "While in bed with my girlfriend, I called her by my ex-girlfriend's name. What do I do?"), and profession-specific questions ("How has being an accordion player improved your sexual technique? And how can a non-accordion player improve the same skills?").

For the sake of our readers (and editors), we kept the lines of inquisition as varied as possible. Still, there was one question we never tired of asking: "What's a sex mistake that you'd like to warn others against?" "Don't assume you know how to use a whip," responded Elvin, a twenty-five-year-old nudist. Ouch. Lashings aside, his response and many others reminded us that imperfect sex is our favorite kind. If everyone got it right the first time, then advice would be unwarranted and sex itself would be a lot less memorable.

With that in mind, we hope you have as much fun reading this book as we had putting it together. Take notes; try a few new toys, techniques, and positions; but for gosh sake don't get too good at it! Your bumbling and fumbling make for better stories, and one of these days we'll get around to interviewing you.

If you have a question that you'd like answered, please e-mail us at sexadvice@nerve.com.

—The Nerve staff

ACCORDION PLAYERS

Michael, 32

🎙 **I just found out that my boyfriend once had sex with a prostitute, and I'm horrified. Is that normal, and is there any way I can get over this?**

Hell, no. Not that I know of. But I'm an accordion player.

🎙 **How much masturbation is too much masturbation, and does it differ for men and women?**

I say the point at which it's too much masturbation is the point at which you've chafed yourself or you can't get it up or get aroused when you truly need to be.

🎙 **What's the best music for putting you in the mood?**

I don't know that any music puts me in the mood. NPR puts me in the mood.

🎙 **You ever use that as a pickup line? "Want to go back to my place and listen to some NPR?"**

"*Car Talk*'s comin' on tonight." Get a bottle of brandy and *Car Talk*. It's better than watching *When Harry Met Sally*.

Susan, 28

🐱 **What's the best music for putting you in the mood?**
Polka? Kidding. Marvin Gaye. I know it sounds tacky. Oh, and Prince. I like Prince a lot.

🐱 **It's the assless pants.**
It's weird. He's not that attractive. He's small and girly looking, with his big girly eyes, but there's something about him that makes you want to do stuff with him.

🐱 **What's the hottest nonporn movie to impress a date with?**
Free Willy, just because it has Michael Maxon in it. I don't date that much. Then there's *Henry and June.* It has a lot of girl-on-girl action, and you also get to see Uma Thurman's tits. But you get to see Uma Thurman's tits in a lot of movies.

🐱 **My new girlfriend is bi. She loves me but she wants me to bring a man into the bedroom. I want to make her happy, but I'm not totally comfortable with the idea. What should I do?**
I would say try it, but first tell her, "I'm going to try it one time. If I like it, we can try it again. If I don't, then we don't have to do it anymore." It's always a little risky bringing another person into the relationship because all kinds of weird jealousies can happen. But it could develop into a unique situation where you can have multiple partners or multiple gender partners. Or, if he's really lame in bed, you can always say, "See, I'm much better. Stick with me."

My last boyfriend had a signature move that I really want my new boyfriend to try. Do I tell him?

Yes, tell him, tell him, tell him! But don't tell him where you learned it. Or maybe you can help him develop his own thing. Most likely you'll teach him the previous move but you probably want to alter it in a way that makes it his own.

How has being an accordion player improved your sexual technique?

I'm a better multitasker. It's given me upper-body strength because uprights are really heavy. My biggest one is like thirty pounds. You have to learn to do different things with your left and your right, and if you sing, too, then you're doing four things at once. Just in general, eye-hand coordination and manual dexterity with fingers.

How can a non-accordion player improve the same skills?

Learn how to play the accordion or the drums, because you have to do the same thing in terms of doing something different with both hands. And you should practice practice practice.

ACTORS

Caitlin, 19

🐱 What's the most classless thing a guy can do in bed?

Try to slip anal. You know, when you're grinding with a guy and he tries to sneak his dick in your ass. That's just a smidge invasive. And it's happened to me before. It's like our third date and—wait a minute, I don't wanna sound like a whore—twelfth date, and all of a sudden something goes up there and I'm like, "Whoa, no permission, no entry." Something else that's classless is when you're giving head to a guy and . . .

🐱 He puts his hands on your head?

Oh, I don't mind that. That's like a fantasy thing, like he has the power. He doesn't, of course—you could bite his dick off—but he thinks you're being submissive. So where was I? Oh, yeah, if you're giving a guy oral sex and he tries to come in your face. Asking is one thing, but being sneaky about it sucks.

🐱 Under what circumstances is it okay to sleep with somebody to get what you want?

I mean, whatever. Wow, I totally sound like a whore in this interview. But I mean, we've all got our thing, and if you're okay fucking someone to get it, then rock the fuck on.

🐱 Name three things everybody should try at least once.

Everyone should try anal sex at least once. I hesitate to say that one first as I'm not really into it. But I think that it's important because the bum is overlooked, doesn't get enough credit. I think that everybody should try a threesome once and everybody should try a same-gender experience at least once. Doing these things will teach you so much about who you are. You're either going to like it more or less than you thought you would. And that's an important thing to know. I'm three for three, by the way.

Jayme, 29

🐚 **What word should a man never use to refer to your vagina?**

Coochie is fine, *pussy* is fine, *cunt* is fine. Just stay away from references to any and all marine animals.

🐚 **What are some do's and don'ts for making an X-rated home movie?**

Do be okay with at least one other person outside of that relationship seeing you in that way, because, well, somebody will. You can count on it. Years after the fact the person will show a friend, or your mom is visiting and pops it in the VCR. Or, even worse, suppose that you died and friends and family were sorting through everything that you had. Ha ha ha. Actually that would be a funny last way for them to see you. Maybe every wake should feature a shaky ten-minute movie of the person being fucked silly on the dining-room table.

Sean, 19

You have an experience with someone who is a terrible lover. They ask, "How was it for you?" What do you tell them?
Well, if you're dating that person, it would behoove you to tell them what's up. If it's a one-night stand, it's more about helping them and their future sexual partners. I'd say something nice at the same time, though—applaud their effort at least. Try to throw in a subtle hint like "Maybe you shouldn't be doing that to that area, it really hurts" or "That happens to be illegal in all fifty states."

What are some great anal sex tips?
To get it in, think a happy thought and try to relax as best you can. Cleanliness really is right up there with godliness. Third, lubrication. I mean a lot of lube— enough to make sitting on a bar stool a bad idea for fear of swallowing it.

What are some do's and don'ts for hand jobs?
You can't fuck yourself or blow yourself, but you can masturbate, and you're probably pretty good at it, so anyone giving you a hand job has a hard act to follow. With that in mind, I think it's a good idea to get the person to jerk off in front of you. Then, when you take the reins, so to speak, get behind them and do it from the same angle they'd do it themselves.

Sex Advice From

ACUPUNCTURISTS

Dr. Marc Ryan, 42

What's the best food or herbal aphrodisiac?

Deer antler is one of the primary sexual tonics. Most Chinese herb stores carry it, but some of the best quality is at Korean stores. Ginseng is popular. Fish eggs, raspberries, pine nuts, blue-green algae. I recommend fish eggs.

While in bed with my girlfriend, I called her by my ex-girlfriend's name. What do I do?

Say something like "I get very excited having sex and I lose track of basic things I would normally be aware of. I'm in the alpha state." You can't control what's coming out of your mouth.

What about group sex? Does ancient Oriental medicine have a position on it? What's the most important rule?

Do what your mom taught you. Be polite. Say please and thank you.

Dr. E. Reenah McGill, 65

🐱 **What's the most effective acupuncture treatment for treating a low sex drive?**
It's usually a combination of acupuncture and herbs—a lot of times people have low chi and don't have enough energy to do anything. It could be depression, liver fire, or liver yang rising, or kidney yin deficiency. I have five positions—two of the needles pointed in toward the testes around the pubic area . . .

🐱 **You actually put the needles in the testes? That sounds painful.**
Actually, it's not. Two needles point in and two point up and in, and one right in the center, down an inch from the pubic bone. I may add points to the hands, the head, and the feet.

🐱 **What's the most erotic nongenital pressure point?**
If you go about four inches up from the tailbone along the spine, there's a spot called Mingmen, and that's the kidney fire point.

🐱 **What's a good food or herbal aphrodisiac?**
For herbs, it's a combination. There's yohimbe, there's horny goat weed, and those are the two you see the most often. Chocolate seems to work the best as a food.

🐱 **What about group sex? Does ancient Oriental medicine have a position on it? What's the most important rule?**
Don't stare. It makes other people uncomfortable. And smile. Say what you're name is. "Hi, I'm Reenah." If they have a beautiful body, there's no reason you shouldn't say so. But don't stare. You'll look like an amateur.

Dr. Felice Dunas, fortysomething

What's the most effective acupuncture treatment for treating a low sex drive?
There isn't a single one. Acupuncture is customized for each patient, and for each session. Generally, people take their life force and use it for other things, so that there isn't enough left to create a healthy sex drive. In traditional Oriental medicine, the internal organs of the body are regarded very differently than they would be by your physician. For example, the liver is responsible for regulating the flow of emotion, whereas the kidney regulates a person's underlying strength that allows for mental capacity and conception. That's why when you're mentally stressed you don't feel sexual, and it's why when you're in bed you're really stupid.

Is it possible to dissipate your chi and bring about an early death by having too much sex?
Don't have sex when you're tired. Sometimes people feel aroused when they're tired, but that desire level can actually come from the body trying to point out that it's tired.

What's the most erotic nongenital pressure point?
There are points on the inside of the calf that have a direct connection to the genitals.

Sex Advice From

ASPIRING
CHIPPENDALES

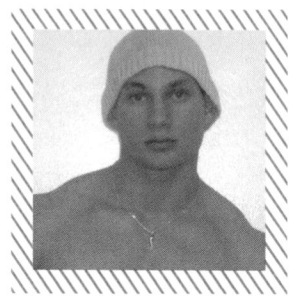

Sean, 23

What's a common mistake people make when trying to dance seductively (see Elaine's "full-body dry heave" from *Seinfeld*)?

If it looks like they're trying, if they're in their head instead of getting in touch with their body, then it's not sexy.

Pubic grooming: what length/formation is best?

On women, if I had to choose, I would say all the way.

My boyfriend is really self-conscious about his body. Do you have any tips for how I can make him feel better about it in the bedroom?

Tell him how much you love how his body feels against yours. It's not all about six-pack abs. Just let him know you really appreciate how he makes you feel.

What position is best for a quick orgasm?

I would say a quick female orgasm would be doggy style. For male orgasm, the girl's lying on the bed and the guy is on his knees or on the floor and the girl's legs are up in the air.

What are some tips for picking up a stripper/dancer?

I'm not sure, I'm not a Chippendale yet. But I would say don't act like a crazed fan. Act like you see him as any other man you're attracted to. Not somebody who was just stripping down to a g-string on stage.

Prince, 22

What are the do's and don'ts of stripping as foreplay?

For the ladies, high heels are a definite do. When I strip in the bedroom, I start with some nice boxers and work boots and work my way down from there. It needs to be dark. You have to have that nice mood light, then come out to some R. Kelly.

A no-fail technique to delay ejaculation?

I pray.

You pray to God?

I know, it's really bad.

What sounds should you make in bed?

It depends on what type of sex you're having. If you're fucking, grunt or do whatever you need to do. If you're making love, take it to the next level. I just think it's important to sleep with people who aren't afraid to let loose in bed. Sometimes I want to talk; sometimes I want a girl to slap me, tell me I'm an asshole. I like stuff like that. It gets you more excited.

What's the best music for getting in the mood?

I like a little Sade. Then I'll move into some R&B: R. Kelly, a little Jill Scott. I can't really have sex to pop music. It's too competitive. I also can't have sex with the TV on.

What's the best position for a quick female orgasm? And what's the best position for a quick male orgasm?

My favorite position is when her legs are up and I'm going at it from the front. Most of the women I've dated enjoyed that as well. It's quick, it's easy, and then you can get back to work.

My boyfriend never instigates sex, and I always end up making the first move. How do I get him to be more proactive?

Look sexy. A lot of women are upset when men don't want sex. But you might be walking around without your hair done, without any makeup, without heels. Make your man want you. Show up at his work in a nice skirt. If you don't know what sexy is, just look at the pop stars, girls like Beyoncé. And then, if he's still not looking at you, communicate with him.

Rob G., 29

What are the do's and don'ts of stripping as foreplay? What should women wear, what should men wear, etc.?

Skirts and high heels for a woman—very classy. For a man, tank tops and tear-away pants.

Male bisexuality: myth or reality?

Being in this entertainment field, it is definitely a reality.

Female ejaculation: Have you experienced it? How do you make it happen?

First of all, you gotta last. Take your time, change positions. When you're penetrating, make sure you hit it from the right angle. Every woman is different, and you've got to know where the woman's G-spot is. Some women like penetration along with finger stimulation. Some like just penetration. Some like it really deep and hard. Some like it deep and rotating. You've just got to really feel your woman out. Once you know what she likes, keep up the hard work and she'll produce.

How can a woman give the perfect blow job?

You have to go down on the entire shaft. As you're doing it, jerk him off with your hand. With the opposite hand, massage the testicles. That is an amazing blow job. And you gotta be sure to lubricate your hand or spit on his shaft. Otherwise you're going to yank his skin, and it's going to be horrible.

What are some tips for picking up a stripper/dancer?

If you're really attracted to an entertainer—not necessarily a dancer or a stripper—you can't be so forward. You've gotta give them something to strive for. Every girl out there is throwing it at them. Be different. Stand out.

Isaiah, 20

🎤 **Have you ever encountered any interesting pubic grooming?**
She shaved it in the shape of a strawberry. Another time she shaved it like a star. Lucky Charms, I guess.

🎤 **What sounds should you make in bed?**
"Yes" is always good. "Oh my God" is always good. I say bring God into the bedroom. I'm pretty silent, a bit of a breather. I'm known to growl every now and then. The ladies love the growl.

🎤 **What's the best position for a quick female orgasm? And what's the best position for a quick male orgasm?**
Missionary with a pelvic angle, angling her kind of up with a pillow underneath her. And for me personally, doggy style. I'm a doggy-style fan.

🎤 **Is there such a thing as watching too much porn? How much porn is too much?**
[*Laughs*] When you can sit down to your pornography with a meal. I had a roommate in college who watched it like it was the ten o'clock news. Sitting there, legs crossed, plate of spaghetti, watching porn.

🎤 **What are some tips you have for someone who wants to give the perfect blow job?**
Keep the teeth above the waist. Get a nice tight vacuum going on. Practice on your thumb. If it feels good to you, it would probably feel good for him.

🎤 **What are some tips for picking up a stripper or a dancer?**
Say, "I'd like to see you with your clothes on."

BIKE
MESSENGERS

Mike, 30

What's the most humane way to tell someone "We've been fucking for two weeks, but it's just not working out"?
Take her out with a bunch of your friends. Get her really drunk, then tell her you're not into it, but you have a bunch of single friends who might be.

Have you ever reenacted a sex scene from a film?
There's this freaky French bondage movie *Story of O*. That's a good one! Women actually really like it. I tied one girl to the door and did naughty things to her.

Tips for sex in public or on wheels?
Stairwells are good. So are freight elevators, the ones that are manually operated. As for sex on wheels, you can do it on certain bikes. I have a friend who has a cargo bike. You could put a bed on the front of that bike and two people could do it while he rode around, but on a regular bike it would be pretty tricky. Maybe you could work something out on a tandem bike, with one person in front of the other. A three-wheeled bike would work, too.

Stacy, 24

🐱 **Have you ever reenacted a sex scene from a film?**

Not consciously, no. But I would like to try the scene from *Y Tu Mamá También* where there's this older woman and she has these two guys on a road trip. One of them comes out of the shower in a towel and she pretty much seduces him. He's nervous, and it's a good scene.

🐱 **Your girlfriend/boyfriend wants sex twice as much as you do. How do you deal?**

I used to try and just avoid it, fall asleep early, talk about how tired I am. Now I just tell him, "You know what, I can't be on it right now, I can't do it." That seems to work a lot better than the other tactic.

🐱 **My boyfriend won't allow me to kiss him the morning before he's brushed his teeth, even though I've told him it doesn't matter. He won't have sex or go down on me unless we've both had a shower. His hygiene obsession is killing the mood. What do I do?**

Pin him down enough times so that he feels comfortable! My boyfriend is kind of shy about that in the morning, but he got over it after I forced him to give me a kiss in the morning. I feel like if he's really into the relationship, who cares? There's something sweet about it when you're both sleepy and disheveled.

Massamba, 24

What's the most humane way to extricate yourself from a one-night stand in the middle of the night?

I would tell her that I have to pick up my uncle who's coming from Senegal, that I have to go to the airport. If it's the next morning, you could still say you have to go meet your uncle who's coming from overseas and doesn't speak English, doesn't know anything about America.

I have an STD that hardly ever flares up. When should I tell a potential sexual partner?

You have to tell them that first night, by the end of the date. You have to lay it out there. Once you start touching, and you feel the person getting a bit over the edge, you have to say what's up. Don't just let this thing slide. If there's no touching at all, there's no need to say anything. That person might not be interested in you.

How do you pick up a bike messenger?

Say things like "You're in shape," "Looking good," "I like your shoes," anything! Girls say, "You have a nice body," or "I like your face/complexion/smile/your helmet/your shades!" They're just trying to start conversation. It's not too hard.

Sex Advice From

BLOGGERS

Jessica, 25

What's hotter: snarkiness or detached irony?

[*Laughs.*] Let's say detached irony, because if I hear the word "snarky" one more time I'm gonna, like, slit my wrists and spray my blood all over Manhattan. I cannot stand that word!

Does detached irony work equally well for men and women?

Well, you know, detached irony in men becomes this disaffected-disillusioned-guy thing—misunderstood, angry poet man or whatever. I'm not sure it comes off the same way. But there's something kind of sexy about a jaded woman. But not a worn woman.

What are some tips for making a home video worthy of being leaked on the Internet?

First of all, be as unattractive as possible, because people LOVE that. They have to see you looking your worst. It's sad, but it's true. Make sure you're holding the handheld yourself. People tend to want that angle. Say a lot of really dumb stuff—the more embarrassing it is, the better it is for the Internet. Also, make sure your partner (if you're the more famous person) is totally anonymous. So everyone's like, "Who the fuck is that?" And have lots of really nasty close-ups.

My boyfriend is freaky tall and I'm freaky not. Is there a sex position that would put us crotch to crotch but also face to face?

I've always had a problem with that because I'm really short and I've always dated really tall guys. Face to face and crotch to crotch, I think probably the best thing is him sitting on the couch and you getting on top.

Perez, 27

What are some tips for leading a sex life that's more like a celebrity's?

Always have a camera handy. Always have a few lesbians programmed in your cell phone. Or bisexual girls, they're interchangeable. Make sure your drug dealer delivers. Have your Viagra—fuck Viagra, that's for losers—have your Cialis prescription by the bed.

What are some tips for making a home video worthy of being leaked on the Internet?

You need to have more than one scene. It's got to be somewhat professional, you know? Professionally amateur. If you look at the Paris video, the Chyna video, or the Pamela Anderson video, there were several scenes strung together. You really have to commit to it. If you could even afford a director or cinematographer to help you, that would be great. Craigslist comes in very handy.

What's the best public place to get busy?

The roof of your apartment building. Everybody's done that. If you haven't done it, you're missing out.

What public place is cliché?
A taxicab. If you're gonna do it in any moving vehicle you might as well do it in one of those carriages in Central Park. At least then you could incorporate the horse in it somehow.

What's the best way to get a blogger to go home with you?
Tempt them with some advertising. Seriously.

Jonno, 37

My significant other of two years just started working out, dressing differently, and initiating more sex. I think this makeover was inspired by a hottie at work, and I just happen to be reaping the benefits. Should I just take them with a smile? Should I ask about it? Should I do anything else?

You should enjoy it, but you should probably also start working out and dressing better. A little healthy competition, if that's the right word, is a good thing in any relationship. As someone who gained maybe twenty pounds in the first year of my relationship . . . um, yeah, I've been there.

How can I disguise or diminish BDSM marks?

I think anything that's supposed to work for hickeys works for BDSM marks. So, the old cold spoon on the neck. Put a spoon in the freezer for a little while, then press the back of the spoon against the bruise. It's just another kind of cold compress. But it actually does work.

Chris, 21

What are some tips for making a home video worthy of being leaked on the Internet?

Being leaked on. R. Kelly found that out the hard way. I would say if you want to get leaked, you really might literally have to be leaked on.

What guidelines should I set up with my partner before making a sex tape?

I think a lot of guys, if they have a partner who's consenting to something like that, might think all bets are off and they can make whatever they're watching on their computer at night. You should probably lay down ground rules: "Please don't pull my hair out." "Please don't slap me in the face with your dick" (which I think is a favorite). Stuff like that.

What are the rules on kissing someone after giving them head?

I guess it's a personal preference. I know dudes who will storm out of the room angry if a girl tries to kiss them afterward. That's not cool. She put in some work down there.

What about after licking ass?

That might be a little different. But you know, if they're willing to do that for you, you could give them a little peck afterward.

Sex Advice From

BODYBUILDERS

Christine, 32

What are some of the sexual benefits of becoming a body-builder?

There are heaps of benefits. Generally there are more men involved in the sport than women, so there is a good male/female ratio, which increases your chances of meeting guys. Most of the people you meet at the gym are in better shape and happier with their bodies, so they're more sexually confident. Muscle control is increased with weight training, which has huge benefits with being able to control orgasms.

What's the most undervalued muscle for sex?

Abdominal muscles, without a doubt. For women, being able to hold an isometric contraction can be critical to reaching an orgasm during sex.

What is the sexiest body part?

I'm a sucker for lean, vascular forearms.

Any exercise videos that will get me in shape and in the mood?

Try watching my training video: *Christine Envall—Superfreak.*

Ray, a.k.a. Stingray, 30

Is it ever okay to hook up with your trainer?

I typically try to maintain a strictly business relationship with my female clients, although there have been a couple of "special" ones. There was this one girl that I trained last year. She once offered to undress so I could "check her fat." I didn't oblige. But soon enough, one thing led to another . . .

What do the following fitness routines say about a person's sexual characteristics:

• A woman who only takes yoga and pilates?
Sexually frustrated, likes gentle sex.

• A guy who goes on long runs alone?
Sexually frustrated, not getting enough.

• A female bodybuilder?
Definitely sexually frustrated! Not enough sex at home so she had to find peace at the gym.

Who isn't sexually frustrated in your book? What about the regulars at cardio striptease class?

They're not getting enough sex at home, and they like foreplay and watching pornos while having sex.

What workout gear could double as bedroom paraphernalia?

Have your partner lay down on a medicine ball with their legs spread open.

Eryk, 34

 Are there any exercises I can get my boyfriend to do to improve his libido?

Performing "forced reps" is great for the libido. These are repetitions that require a spotter. That can be you. Having him aggressively squeeze out the last "forced reps" with your help will cause his body to kick out testosterone. Testosterone is directly related to sexual desire.

How do you tell your lover the following:

• Their body needs some serious toning?

Be proactive in your suggestions. Don't just tell them to work out. Go out there and work out with them. Be a team, because I'm sure there are things your partner doesn't like about you. Treat others, especially your lover, with the same respect and sensitivity you'd like to be treated with.

• Their oral sex technique needs improving?

Again, be proactive. I masturbate in front of my girlfriend because it turns her on and tells her where I am most sensitive. It turns me on when my girlfriend lets me know either with a moan or a verbal reply that I've done something to give her the tingles.

What are some good pickup lines to use at the gym?

Would you mind if I shared your bench? Can you actually feel that movement? Can you show me what I am doing wrong? What competition are you getting ready for?

What workout gear could double as bedroom paraphernalia?

An inclinable weight bench is all you need. Although I enjoy wearing a jockstrap in the bedroom, because it shows off my ass.

Sex Advice From

COLLEGE STUDENTS

Lenny, 18

A date tells you he or she wants to try water sports. Do you dare or do you dump?
Definitely dare.

You know what "water sports" are, right?
What are they?

Urination.
Never mind, then.

What's the best way to initiate a first kiss?
Definitely don't make any statements like "Okay, I'm going to kiss you now."

Is it okay to have anal sex on a first date?
Unless you really see yourself having any kind of future with that person, or if you're just really intoxicatingly drunk, in which case I'm going to say no.

Mariah, 20

🐱 **A date tells you he or she wants to try water sports. Do you dare or do you dump?**
Totally do it! Water sports? Yeah, that's fun! Why wouldn't you?

🐱 **Do you know what "water sports" refers to?**
Like, waterskiing.

🐱 **No, it's urinating.**
Oh. I would do it.

🐱 **You would?**
Well, I wouldn't let them urinate in my mouth, and I would make sure I didn't have any open cuts that are bleeding.

🐱 **My friend says she can only orgasm when she's by herself. How can she loosen up when she's hooking up?**
Try masturbating with someone. And tell her partner what she likes about being with herself and then work from there.

🐱 **Is there such a thing as a successful pickup line?**
Probably not, unless it's "Can I buy you a drink?"

So if someone does buy you a drink, do you owe them anything?

Yeah, I think you owe them a little bit of conversation. Just a little bit. If it gets uncomfortable, just say, "No, thank you." That's essentially the same as saying, "I'm through with you." Because, you know, you don't have to take the drink.

What's the best position for quickest mutual orgasm?

From behind, I'd say. Or actually, no, sort of lying on your stomach, and him on top.

What's the best position for female satisfaction?

Well, that all depends. I like 69 a lot, but that's very intimate. I guess it depends on whether you feel like really getting the spiritual experience. Physically, 69 is the best one. Oh, another one is legs-over-the-shoulders. I don't know what that one's called, though.

Sex Advice From

COMPETITIVE EATERS

Crazy Legs, 34

Hand jobs—do people actually give these anymore?

When I was a short-order cook, for some reason all the women that I hooked up with gave me hand jobs. Getting a hand job in a public place raises the bar a little.

My boyfriend "finishes" too fast in bed. What can I do to help him slow things down?

A lot of competitive eaters are sprinters—they get out of the gate too fast and suffer an "urge contrary to swallowing." There's a parallel there with guys who move too fast during sex and suffering premature ejaculation. You really need to set a pace for yourself and try to keep that pace, whether you're in a baked-bean-eating contest or you're making love.

Patreesha, 20

🐱 What skills are a help in the bedroom?
Honestly, I don't think I have a functional gag reflex anymore. Spit or swallow?
Spitting means you're disqualified!

🐱 Should food be incorporated into sex/foreplay? If so, how?
Not to be closed-minded or anything, but I don't want a man to be eating a
peeled banana out of my ass. Also, if you like big, burly, manly men like I do, you
should know that whipped cream or chocolate syrup and copious amounts of body
hair just do not mix.

🐱 What are the keys to a perfect hand job?
Don't choke it, stroke it, and give those poor twins some attention.

🐱 What are the rules for being a fuck buddy?
A friend of mine told me recently, "The Fuck Buddy Club is like the U.S. Senate—
most people don't get in, and the ones that do aren't sure how they got there.
They're both exclusive, but the difference is that they pass laws and we hump.
Don't make a big deal out of it, and you'll keep coming back term after term."

Tim, 28

How does being a competitive eater enhance your sex life? What skills are a help in the bedroom?

In an eating contest you hit the wall right around five or six minutes, depending on what you're eating. At that point you're trying to figure out "How can I last?" The same thing happens during sex. The trick is to figure out how in your mind you can overcome the urge to quit. The same sort of willpower comes into play.

What are the rules for being a fuck buddy? How do you know the line has been crossed and she wants something more?

When she starts getting angry at you—that's the line. I never have arguments with my real friends. If a fuck buddy's doing that, she's not really your buddy anymore.

What food reminds you most of the male anatomy?

Fugu. It's a poisonous puffer fish from Japan. You can die from eating it. But it increases in size, so I guess that'd be it.

What about the female anatomy?

Pudding. It's amorphous; you can't really figure out where the center is. I love pudding, but it's tough to comprehend. It's all sorts of things.

Sex Advice From

COMPOSERS

Stephen, 27, composer, *Slut*

🎤 **Let's say you had a first date that went really well. How do you orchestrate a perfect second date?**
I think the way to orchestrate the second date is to take some piece of information that you've gleaned on that first date and spin that for your second date. So if you find out that the person you're with happens to be a big fan of freshly made guacamole, surprise them by taking them to Guacamoleville, the Finest Guacamole in All of Manhattan. You should use whatever it is you've learned and come up with something of interest to your partner.

🎤 **I'm totally loyal to my boyfriend, but I like to get off by fantasizing about other men. Is there a way for me to share my fantasies with my boyfriend that will not make him feel insecure or jealous, but bring us closer?**
No. Don't share them. They're your fantasies. Why is your boyfriend going to get turned on by the fact that you're thinking about Matt Damon when you fuck him? So when you're ready to have a shared fantasy, sit down and maybe you can figure something out.

🎤 **What's the best way to get a composer to come home with you after a concert?**
Be a producer.

Bob, 52

What's the best instrument to learn if you're looking to vent some sexual frustration?

Oh, drums! Which is why women are drawn to drummers the same way they're drawn to dangerous men.

Let's say you had a first date that went really well. How do you orchestrate a perfect second date?

Don't try to go too fast. It's all about shutting up and listening. If you tried to be a good listener on the first date, try to be a better listener on the second date.

I love my fiancé but he has no clue what to do with his hands while we're having sex. Is there anything I could suggest to him that might save our sex life?

This is why women love piano players. Piano players always know what to do with their hands. Men are so genital oriented that they forget what women want, which is not to say that they shouldn't focus on the genitals, but it's more about the full body. Lightly caress the neck. Most men tend to go right to the nipples—forget the nipples. Caress around the outside. Go to either side of the clit. The whole area is erogenous.

Is cheating inevitable?

Almost. I don't believe that any human being can belong to anyone else. What you do is you make a promise that you're not going to mess around with anyone else, for whatever reason. And it's all about keeping your promise. So far I've kept my promise to my wife and she's kept it to me. That doesn't mean I don't want to cheat—please, constantly. And any man who says different is lying.

A good friend of mine has a huge crush on me, by his own admission. I have never been physically attracted to him. However, I could totally see him being the perfect boyfriend. Should I go for it?

That's a tough one because my wife and I started out disliking each other, so yeah, it's possible, sure. Sometimes in my life, the relationships that I've been the hottest with ended because we had absolutely nothing in common, and as soon as we got out of bed we had nothing to say to each other. In the end, it's always good to go with a slow burn rather than a quick fire.

David, 30

🎤 **I've been single for about a year now and I've finally met a guy I really like. My last relationship ended terribly so I'm still a little twitchy when it comes to men. I'm so afraid of being rejected that every time my new guy waits a couple of days to call, I start panicking. I'm afraid I'm going to scare him away with my insecurities and neurosis. Is this normal? How can I keep from freaking out and scaring him away?**

A good rule of thumb is, every time you get the urge to call or text or e-mail, deny the urge three out of four times. This should not be considered "playing the game"; it's called pacing yourself. If you want something to last, take time to let things breathe. Your fears are probably mirrored by the other person who is sitting at home denying the urge to call you three out of four times.

🎤 **What's the best music for getting you and someone else in the mood? How about the best music for having sex? Any specific classical music that's good for sex?**

You're really lucky if you find a piece of music or a CD that involves some low, calm songs with an occasional rough-voiced female humming a counterpoint to the brass.

My friend is in a long-term relationship and has only had sex with two people. This bothers her. Should she have sex with others so she knows she isn't missing anything?

I am a firm believer in getting everything out of your system before seeking a relationship. By entering into a relationship, you should be saying, "I have been good to myself and now I am ready to be good for someone else." Plus, practice makes . . . better.

I like BDSM play, and I like it a little rough. My new boy-friend doesn't mind tying me up or blindfolding me—but if I ask for a spanking or a gentle slap, he freaks out. He's not comfortable with the idea of hurting me, even though it's what gets me off. Help?

You need to sit down and have a chat about your boundaries. Let him know that your goal line is a little farther out than your average Joe's. It's, say, thirty feet past the field goal. And for him to make a freakin' touchdown, he's gonna have to step up to the line.

I'm engaged, but my high school crush just e-mailed me out of the blue and wants to get together. I've been fantasizing about this woman since eighth grade! Can I cheat on my fiancée, just this once?

If you do, you're not ready to *have* a fiancée.

CONSTRUCTION WORKERS

Shaun, 26

In bed, how much noise is too much?
Oh, there's never too much noise, ever. Never ever ever.

My boyfriend is a spoiled baby when it comes to oral sex. I go down on him every day, but when I ask him to reciprocate he says, "Someday."
You need to get another boyfriend—that's retarded! Any guy who doesn't like to go down on a girl is from another planet, as far as I'm concerned.

What is the best position for performing oral sex on a woman?
Sit on my face and tell me you love me.

How do you manage sex in the shower when the guy's taller than the girl?
Pick her up. She can put her feet up on the side of the tub, too, but you pick her right up.

I'm looking for tips on the lost art of the hand job.
The key is definitely moisture. Make it slide. None of this fucking sandpaper action. That pull and tug makes you want to say, "All right, sweetie, stop. Leave it alone, please, you're breaking it."

Brady, 30

What's the ideal situation in which to initiate a first kiss?
When the time's right, I usually ask. It might seem kind of cold, but it's always better to ask than go in and get the "ugaah!" It's significantly less embarrassing to say, "Is it all right if I kiss you?"

What is the best position for performing oral sex on a woman?
I've always been a big fan of the 69 thing.

What's the most tantalizing article of clothing for your partner to keep on during sex?
High heels. Boots, mostly. Black leather. They can get a little dangerous though.

How so?
Oh, getting hit in the head—things of that nature.

How many dates would you suggest a woman wait before jumping into bed with someone new?
Dates? How about an hour or so after you meet them? No, two or three weeks is good. Otherwise, you end up having sex with somebody too early. Then there's no mystery and you spend time getting to know each other and all you want to do is have sex. Or else you spend all your time having sex just because you know you can.

Which would be hardest for you to go without for a year: oral sex, penetration, or beer?
Probably beer. Masturbation simulates sex better than nonalcoholic beer simulates beer.

Harrison, 32

What's the best way to touch a nipple?
Very softly. No pinching, no squeezing. Unless it's requested.

My boyfriend is a spoiled baby when it comes to oral sex. I go down on him every day, but when I ask him to reciprocate, he only says, "Someday." How can I make "someday" come sooner?
You simply stop. Don't give it to him anymore. That's ridiculous.

Is it sexy when a thong shows out the back of a woman's pants?
Yeah, but it's much cooler if it happens when you're bending over to pick up your napkin or something. Then it feels like a special treat.

What's the most tantalizing article of clothing to keep on during sex?
A collar or something. Nothing that will inflict pain, but maybe something with a little black leather. Something a little dirty.

Share some tips on the lost art of the hand job.
Women don't realize that the grip is always tighter than you think. Probably go a little quicker. And use two hands, definitely. One for—I just watched *Old School,* so—one for the "stepchildren."

Sex Advice From

COSTUME SHOP EMPLOYEES

Alita, 19   Arman, 24

🐱 **What's the best costume for a man looking to get laid?**

Alita: The gangster costume is pretty hot.

Arman: If you're a muscular guy, you go with something with less coverage. If you're into music, do some makeup, some rock star stuff. I'm going the KISS route this Halloween.

🐱 **A woman looking to get laid?**

Alita: It's gotta be either Elvira or the French maid.

Arman: I like the maids. The skimpier the better.

🐱 **A couple on their first date?**

Alita: There's the nut and the bolt that screw together.

🐱 **How can you casually ask someone if they've been tested for STDs?**

Alita: In a completely casual setting, in a conversation during the course of the day, in a completely different context than the bedroom.

Arman: When I was younger, I used to hint, but as I got older and more paranoid I just went straight out, "Do you have AIDS?"

Stitch, 25

🔥 **I went too far with a guy on a first date. How can I take a step back now without giving him a speech about "slowing down" or "gaining respect"?**

You can just be honest and say, "I really like you, but I don't want a relationship if it's going to be based solely on sex. What happened was initial lust, but I'd really like to get to know you as a friend or companion and actually try to base the relationship on that instead of basing a relationship completely on lustful sex that really doesn't have any emotional ties to it."

🔥 **How can you casually ask someone if they've been tested for STDs?**

You could say, "A friend of mine found out they're HIV positive. It was really upsetting. You know, I was tested about six months ago and I found out that I didn't have anything. Have you ever been tested before?"

🔥 **My boyfriend takes forever to come. Any tips to make it happen faster? Or should I bring it up? If so, how?**

Always have lube handy. It's very good regardless of what you're doing. You can use your finger—make sure your nails are cut—and while you're giving him a blow job, or even during penetration, you gently slide a lubed finger up his ass and massage the prostate gland.

After my girlfriend and I have sex, I always try to get her to talk about what felt good, but she won't give me specifics. How do I get her to communicate?

Share an intimate experience with her. Together you could take your clothes off and masturbate for her. Discuss things while you're having sex to make it a little bit more open.

What is a good scary movie to rent that will get you laid?

I've always been a fan of *Nightmare on Elm Street.*

COWBOYS

Larry, 47

Why do women like country guys?
'Cause city guys is pansies, mostly.

What's a no-fail seduction line?
I dunno. Probably "Let me show you my fingers." [*Holds up two remaining fingers on his left hand.*]

That works?
It has done.

How would you react if a woman asked to penetrate you with a strap-on?
I'd grab my gun. If she was using it on her girlfriend, that would be a different story entirely. But on me? Well shit, man, that just ain't gonna fly.

Tom, 59

Where's the best place to engage in outdoor sex?

Just about anywhere. I've done it in the creek, I've done it on horse blankets. I've done it in the long grass, got thorns in my ass. Hell, once I smoothed out pine needles and threw her down right there. Boy, I tell ya, I've done it all outside. On a horse one time, too. I just had her sit on my lap and got the horse in a trot. Shit, man, it worked real good.

What food should a man eat to ensure his virility?

Plenty of steak and eggs. Make sure that the eggs are runny and the steaks bloody. That'll keep the lead in your pencil.

My girlfriend is afraid to try anal sex. How can I encourage her?

Hmm, that's a tricky one. There was this one time I talked this girl into trying it. She said okay, so I'm lickin' her and lickin' her, I got it all juiced up good. Then I go to put it in. I had her underneath me. I poked her pretty hard, 'cause it wasn't goin' in good. She shot right out of my arms, hit her head on the headboard, and said, "That's it." She wouldn't let me do it no more. So I don't know, boy, what can I tell ya? Some of 'em will, some of 'em won't. I guess you just gotta sweet-talk 'em.

Any other words of wisdom?

Well [*crosses arms and looks over yonder*], I'd say patience. Boy, I tell you: you know what they say about it being a virtue? Well, it's true. You just got to lick 'er and slick 'er, then broom-grab her 'til she hollers.

Max, 51

The best place to engage in outdoor sex?

It could be on the hood of a Corvette. See, there's not enough room to have sex on the inside of a Corvette. Those sports cars are too small to get laid in, but you get laid just about as soon as you get out.

How would you react if a woman asked to penetrate you with a strap-on?

Don't listen to those other guys. They'd never admit to it, but I'll bet that if a good-lookin' woman wanted to stick 'em they'd say, "What the hell!" They ain't telling you the whole truth! These motherfuckers lie all the time.

There's the truth, and then there's the truth you wouldn't tell in front of your drinking buddies.

Ain't that the truth!

Sex Advice From

DELI WORKERS

Juan, 29

Have you ever had sex with someone in the deli?
Yes, I do it as often as possible. But it's a busy joint, so finishing is mostly out of the question.

My girlfriend wants to have a threesome with another man, but I'm nervous about that power dynamic. How can I calm my nerves?
Smoke a joint, then smoke a real blunt with my Rastafarian brothers. After you get high, you will have no problem being controlled.

What product do you sell that's best for self-stimulation?
I believe Dawn dish liquid will serve all purposes. It can lube, and the bottle can stimulate. It's definitely a two-in-one.

A friend insists that oysters make him horny. What is the most effective aphrodisiac that you sell?
Horny goat weed. It comes in a package. Let me know if it works.

Antonio, 38

🔥 **Have you ever seen someone have sex in your deli? Did you watch or kick them out?**
Of course I've watched. One time I taped it. I'm thinking of selling it on the Internet.

🔥 **What food item do you sell that would be best for sexual use?**
Mayo. Hellmann's. It's quality.

🔥 **If your dream person came walking into your deli, how would you woo that person under the harsh overhead lighting?**
I would definitely ask them if they had tried our vast selection of meats.

🔥 **How often do you get hit on at work?**
At least once a week. All sorts, too—women, men, every type of person.

🔥 **How can I enhance the size of my penis?**
If it's small, it's small. Live with it. Myths are myths, and it's not going to get any bigger. Sorry!

🔥 **Is it better to be treated tenderly or roughly in bed? Do you ever wear your apron for fun?**
I definitely like it rough. Are you kidding me? An apron? That's entirely out of the question.

🔥 **How many times an hour do you think of sex while working at the deli?**
About five times an hour. Mostly about going home and having sex there.

Joanne, 24

🐱 What is the best aphrodisiac you sell?

We have a pill called Vigora. But we don't sell many of them, because most people just laugh and think they aren't real. But there are some guys who swear by it.

🐱 What's your favorite beer/wine cooler/alcoholic energy drink to get your mate all boozed up?

I have to say mix Red Bull with Guinness. It may not taste that great, but they're gonna get fucked up. People I know do it all the time; they say it works well.

🐱 Do you get hit on at work?

Oh, yeah, it happens all the time. They say all sorts of things like "Oh, you're really pretty," "I like what I see," or "sexy lady." I try not to get mad, but once I slapped a guy. He just kept trying to touch me and take pictures of me, and he's married and has kids! So I slapped him. I don't want that kind of drama in my life.

🐱 How do you retain your sex appeal on the job?

I comb my hair and put on some lipstick and a little makeup. If I'm a little bored and feel kinda sad, I might have a beer.

Sex Advice From

DIPLOMATS

Ethan, 29

In what country or city am I most likely to get laid on a quick vacation?

Sweden. In the same way that Israelis like blondes, Swedes like darker people. When you look different, you get more attention.

If you're single, how do you pick up the hottie sitting next to you on the plane?

Offer them a Mentos or gum. No one's going to turn that down. Also give her your dessert—it's like giving her chocolates on the first date.

Are you a member of the mile-high club?

I'm a five-time member, but you should always claim you're a mile-high virgin. Night flights are the best. Use a blanket.

Are there any exotic positions practiced in other countries that we don't know about stateside?

Come on, in America there is nothing you don't know. The United States is forty times the population of Israel. So I'm sure with all the people here, you haven't missed a thing.

Anne, 32

🐱 **In what country or city am I most likely to get laid on a quick vacation?**

Definitely the Greek islands, like Mykonos and Santorini. Mykonos is a party island, great for men, women, transgenders, whatever. Everyone can find someone on Mykonos.

🐱 **How should you pick up an Italian?**

Well, Italy is all about appearance. Not just expensive fashions like Prada or Dolce—it's about your look. And the look to get the guy is pointy high heels, tight pants, a cleavage-accentuating top. Men are focused on your body. If you look like a high-class slut, you'll get picked up in a minute.

🐱 **If you're single, how do you pick up the hottie sitting next to you on the plane?**

Strike up a conversation about travel. World travel is sexy. Ask them what they're doing at their destination, where they've been. While you're making small talk, order a couple of cocktails and hope it's a long flight!

If you're traveling with your lover, what's the best way to make out with them on a plane or bus without getting caught?
Airline blankets are surprisingly soft, and business-class seats have become really comfortable over the years. During night flights, two people can fit into one business-class seat under a blanket without raising any eyebrows. The best position in the bathroom would be if the guy is standing near the toilet and the woman sits on the counter near the sink. But make it a quickie, and the best time is during the movie when you're less likely to be interrupted.

Sex Advice From

DJs

Leigh, 21

What's the best way to approach someone on the dance floor?

None! Make them approach you! Give eyes from across the room. I'm a big fan of dancing scandalously with all the gay boys. But more often than not, I think that just ends up intimidating a lot of guys. If you don't have the courage to go grab someone and start dancing, just keep drinking until you do.

Do I, in fact, need to lick it before we kick it?

Ooh! A little lick's always a nice starter, but no, it's not necessary. If you're going to do that to me, you have to follow through and take care of me. Guys who'll go down a bit and then take off or fall asleep—it makes me want to fucking cut them.

What qualifies as cheating: flirting, kissing, fooling around, or full-on fucking?

Everything but flirting is cheating.

What's a no-fail cunnilingus technique?

You've got to get your fingers in there. If you're using your mouth and hands simultaneously, that's a sure shot.

What is not an appropriate sound or statement to make at the moment of orgasm?

Anything that's cliché. If someone ever said something like "Who's your daddy?" I'd pretty much jump out of bed, get dressed, and leave. I don't like when people say, "I'm coming." It sounds like bad porn. It's nice when someone says your name or if they compliment you. It's nice to hear "You're so beautiful" or "You're amazing."

Geordan, 21

What's the best way to approach someone on the dance floor?
The best way is not to approach them. It's all about dancing in close proximity, but not too close. You've got to shoot them a few nice, subtle glances. Try to lure them with your eyes.

Do I, in fact, need to lick it before we kick it?
Yes, absolutely. You need to get it soft and wet so we can kick it.

Have you had pleasurable pity sex?
Yes. How about I sum it up in less than ten words? Christian rock. Virgin. Face down, ass up.

What's the biggest mistake a man can make in bed?
Have dry skin. If someone touches me with scaly hands, that's just wrong. And actual tongue penetration of the ear. I also hate when someone kisses anywhere above my lips. It's weird when someone kisses you on the nose. Everything from the lips on down is fine. North of the lips is a no-no.

Sarah, 24

🦋 What's the best way to approach someone on the dance floor?

Saunter over to them while making eye contact. But make sure your eyes are half closed and sexy. You don't want to be wide eyed, like, "I'm staring at you!" Then, when you get near them, just start the dancin'. No words need to be spoken. If you're nervous, it won't work. Guys who approach me halfheartedly always end up getting shot down.

🦋 What's the best way to get the DJ to come home with you?

Offer to help carry their record bags home. Duh.

🦋 Should I tell my girlfriend about my wild sexual past?

No. If they ask you, tell them it's an exaggerated rumor. I make the mistake of telling people everything. I'll be like, "Oh man, you should've seen this thing! Eleven inches!" That's probably why I haven't had a boyfriend in a long time.

🦋 What's the biggest mistake a woman can make in bed?

Not talking dirty to her partner. I used to tell the guy I was dating panty-fantasy stories while we were having sex. He loved it.

🦋 Panty-fantasy stories?

Yeah: "Next time you see me, I want you to bend me over and rip off my panties and take me from behind."

🦋 What's the biggest mistake a man can make in bed?

Moaning too much. Not taking control. There's nothing less sexy than a guy who just lays there. Oh, and insisting on more dirty talk. If I'm done with the dirty talk, don't ask for more.

EDITORIAL ASSISTANTS

Beth, 30

🦇 **I like my boyfriend to call me un-PC names like "slut" and "whore" during sex. He says this makes him feel uncomfortable and hasn't been able to do it. What can I do?**

Tell him you're only going to respond if he addresses you "appropriately," and it might help to explain to him why this is empowering and sexy to you.

🦇 **I have a mad literary crush on Jonathan Franzen. Any tips on getting near famous writers?**

Beware! Avoid! Avoid! Writers are the worst in bed! A pen would make a better lover. But I guess you could try memorizing the dictionary and writing love poetry to them.

Nate, 23

What do the following books say about a person's sexual characteristics?

• A man currently reading *The Da Vinci Code?*
This guy is going to be awful in bed. This is just one step up from a sci-fi reader, someone who thinks sex can't measure up to masturbation.

• A woman reading *He's Just Not That Into You?*
Demanding in bed, no fun at all.

• A woman reading *The Five People You Meet in Heaven?*
I'd say you'd be lucky to get a blow job from her, much less sex.

• A man reading *How to Talk to a Liberal (If You Must)?*
A total kinkmaster. Surprisingly good in bed.

Last week after everyone was gone, a coworker and I ended up getting into some heavy petting in my cubicle. I'd like to become fuck buddies, but now she's ignoring me and acting like nothing happened. Is there a polite way to say, "I'd like to sleep with you with no strings attached"?

No, there's definitely not a polite way to say this. Don't send an e-mail because you don't want this in print. Either call or meet up with them and say, "Are we going to fuck or what?" That should make it clear.

Dan, 23

What do the following books say about a person's sexual characteristics?

- A man currently reading *The Da Vinci Code?*
Dumb slut.

- A woman reading *He's Just Not That Into You?*
Frigid.

- A woman reading *The Five People You Meet in Heaven?*
Enjoys long walks on the beach and curling up in front of the fire to read poetry.

- A man reading *How to Talk to a Liberal (If You Must)?*
Mommy issues.

What books would you recommend I read to get me in the mood? Any passages you'd suggest I read out loud to my lover?
The Sound and the Fury. Pages 1 through 100 are particularly dull. She'll be bored to tears by then and up for anything.

What makes for a good sex scene?
I think the key to any good sex scene in writing is the word "panties." Aggression toward said panties is even better. Also, "throbbing."

What's a surefire way to get an editorial assistant to come home with you?
Buy him or her food. They're all starving. A sweaty wad of cash also works well.

Sex Advice From

EXPATS

Judah, 37, an American living in Provence, France

I want to talk dirty in French to my French boyfriend/girlfriend. What should I say?

I think sex for French people is much more felt than spoken. To be honest, the women who I've had sex with here have not been very talkative, they've been much more sensual and physical. At least I can say there's no language barrier!

One commonly held view about the French is that they're adulterous.

Let's put it this way: French people tend to think of Americans as being very immature when it comes to their expectations about relationships and couples and marriages. The French tend to understand that after twenty years of marriage, it's pretty unlikely there's gonna be a whole lot of sexual passion left. And it's in no one's interest if everyone is really, really miserable because no one's getting any. It's almost "don't ask, don't tell." Just be respectful enough that you don't confront the other person with an unpleasant reality they didn't need to know about.

What about the stereotype that French men and women have bad hygiene?

I have not run into that problem. Just to sort of flip that stereotype, I would say that Americans are probably a little aseptic, a little sterilized. They don't have any body odor at all; it's all washed off or covered up. In France a woman will have the scent of her own skin with a really cool perfume mixed in. This plays into this idea of sex being much more about fussing, mingling, mixing things up. If you don't want to smell the person you're in bed with, what are you doing being in bed with them? Don't you want to feel them, and get a little sweaty and mix things up a little bit?

Teri, 34, an American living in London, England

🐱 Let's talk about what to expect when dating in the UK.

British men think all American girls are as loose as a goose. I guess it's true of anyone who visits another country. You don't have your friends around to judge you, and you aren't around the people you normally see every day, so you can become this fantasy version of yourself. When you're an expat, life's a little more settled than that, but there's still always this element of escaping from your normal life.

🐱 What pickup lines work with Brits?

To be honest, if you're a girl, especially an American girl, you can say anything you want. A chick approaching a guy is so unusual. It's generally not done. They're all so proper and reserved, so if you are a girl approaching a British guy anything you say is an advance. You don't need chat-up lines.

American guys have a trickier time with British women. They're always in groups, so it's this big circle you have to penetrate. You might have to be strategic—wait until one of them leaves the group to order a drink at the bar, and catch them when they're alone.

🐱 What are considered aphrodisiacs in England?

Figs, oysters, and booze.

🐱 Sex in public: what are the best locations in London?

SoHo Square if you can get away with it. It's not very big and it's right in the middle of the West End. There are lots of people around which makes it very risky and exciting. It's locked up at night, so you have to climb over the fence.

Gay men go to Regent's Canal. It's dark and creepy—a real Jack the Ripper vibe. I guess that's part of the thrill. Also Hampstead Heath—that's a major gay pick-up scene at night.

🐱 Where in London would I go to meet someone for a one-night stand?

Leicester Square for all those slutty American tourists. If you want to meet some hot trendy chick, go to any bar in Shoreditch. To meet a rock chick, try one of the small rock clubs: Barfly, Dirty Water, KoKo.

🐱 Someone I can get serious with?

The Victoria and Albert holds these late-night viewings on Fridays and it's a real scene. Or get a reader's ticket for the British Library. There are a lot of hot book-worms there. Get one of them to let her hair down and take off her glasses behind the stacks.

🐱 Someone for an on-the-spot quickie?

There's an occasional giant S&M venue called the Torture Garden. Or do a Web search for swingers. It's SoHo and Vauxhall for the gay cruising scene.

Elizabeth, 40, an American living in Rome, Italy

🐱 Let's talk about what to expect when dating Italians.

There's the stereotype that Italians are the best lovers in the world. They're really good at the approach and flirting but it pretty much stops there. It always turns out that the guy is thirty-five and lives at home with Mother. I could pretty much sum up dating in Italy in three words: Madonna/whore complex. So if you wanna be the whore, you're in there. But you'll never be anything else.

If you really want to fuck an Italian, you should be up for anal sex, because that's the first thing they're going to ask you for. Every single American woman I know here has had this experience. Throw in the fact that they don't want to wear condoms and you've got trouble. So ultimately, they're disappointing.

🐱 What do Italian men think of the Brazilian?

Just make sure you never get a bikini wax from a twenty-five-year-old Italian woman. They will fuck it up on purpose, because they think the first thing you're gonna do is go out and sleep with their boyfriend. They're like, "Oh—is it crooked? Sorry."

🐱 What pickup lines work with Italians?

Italians all smoke. They always come up and say, "Will you offer me a cigarette?" It's a very convenient way to start a conversation with someone. Even if you don't smoke, carry a pack of cigarettes around. Or a lighter.

🐱 I want to talk dirty in Italian. What should I say?

There's a phrase in Italian that just means "What are we doing?"—_"Che facciamo?"_ But if you phrase it slightly differently, "What would we like to do?"—_"Cosa vogliamo fare?"_—it implies that you're referring to sex.

Where in Rome would I go to meet someone for a one-night stand?

They really like the pubs; strangely, they really like Irish pubs. There's a whole club scene as well, in this neighborhood called Testaccio—that's a good place to pick up people. It's not in the guidebooks. Go to a bar called Bar Del Fico.

Someone I can get serious with?

Try an art opening, or a museum. Go to this piazza called Campo Dei, right in the center of Rome and all along the square there are different bars and cafes. By eleven at night, there are hundreds of young beautiful people standing around holding their drinks just chatting each other up. The draw of this place is that the locals really love it.

Someone for an on-the-spot quickie?

If you're a gay man, you go to the park. One is the Villa Borghese; it's a huge park up above the Spanish Steps. That one seems a little more dodgy. There's a park called Monte Caprino that is near the back side of the Roman Forum, and that's really famous for picking up, getting a blow job, whatever. And then there are lots of after-hours gay clubs, a lot of saunas with dark rooms in the back. A lot of options.

Sex in public: what are the best locations in Rome?

Anywhere. Any street, any café, any fountain, any set of steps. So many men live at home with their moms that you have to do it out in the street. Or drive up to La Gianicolo, which has this incredible view of all of Rome. In the summertime you see a lot of parked cars with newspaper in the windows sort of . . . moving.

FEMALE BARTENDERS

Kim, 34

🐱 **What sexual tendencies or characteristics do you associate with the following:**

• A man who orders a chocolate martini?
He's gay.

• A man who orders a dirty martini?
Salty spunk!

• A woman who orders a Maker's Mark, neat?
I love her—she's a badass, confident, maybe a little dominant.

• A woman who orders a Stoli vanilla and Diet Coke?
Mmm, timid.

🐱 **If you had to use one item from behind the bar during sex, what would it be and how would you use it?**
This is pretty awful, but I just thought of the Galliano bottle! Maybe a little bit of whipped cream.

🐱 **Give me some do's and don'ts for a guy who wants to seduce his barmaid.**
Don't use a line, don't lurk too long, and don't get sloppy drunk.

Lucy, 32

What sexual tendencies or characteristics do you associate with the following:

• A man who orders a chocolate martini?
He's a Wall Streeter.

• A man who orders a dirty martini?
Middle-aged, and a gentleman.

• A woman who orders a Maker's Mark, neat?
My kind of girl, no bullshit. But that's my drink, so I'm biased.

• A woman who orders a Stoli vanilla and Diet Coke?
She's probably twenty-two years old and high maintenance!

If you had to use an item from behind the bar during sex, what would it be and how would you use it?
Chambord. It's tasty, it's sweet, it's sticky.

Lydia, 25

🦇 **What sexual tendencies or characteristics do you associate with the following:**

• A man who orders a chocolate martini?
You don't want to jump to the conclusion that he's gay, but it's hard not to. If he's not, I give him a lot of credit for having the gumption to order one.

• A man who orders a dirty martini?
I guess there's something to be said for a man who likes it salty.

• A woman who orders a Maker's Mark, neat?
That woman ain't messin' around. She's a force to be reckoned with.

• What if she orders a Stoli vanilla and Diet Coke?
I don't understand the concept of mixing vodka with Coca-Cola.

🦇 **If you had to use one item from behind the bar during sex, what would it be and how would you use it?**
A muddler! It's a wooden stick that you use to mash stuff in a bowl and it kind of looks like a baseball bat. There are many ways that you could use that.

Delilah, 35

What is the worst attempted pickup you ever witnessed from behind the bar?

All the old clichés like "Do I know you from somewhere?" But there's nothing worse than a woman who's just hanging on a man and won't take no for an answer. It's very rare that I see a guy who's physically clinging to a woman, but women think they have a right to touch other people.

What sexual tendencies or characteristics do you associate with the following:

• A man who orders a chocolate martini?
Oh, he's gay.

• What if it's a dirty martini?
He's a real confident man. It's a tough drink.

• A woman who orders Maker's Mark, neat?
Also a tough drink. For a strong personality.

• And if she orders Stoli vanilla and Diet Coke?
Oh, please! Are you joking?

🐱 If you had to use one item from behind the bar during sex, what would it be and how would you use it?

The first one would be ice. We also have candles behind the bar, so you could use wax.

🐱 Give me some do's and don'ts for a guy who wants to seduce his barmaid.

Bartenders flirt, but it's a business, and 90 percent of the time it's done because money is involved.

Sex Advice From

FEMALE MODELS

Elisa Anna, 22

What can normal folks like us do to bed a model?

A lot of my friends date "normal guys," but with the exception of the guy I'm with now, I really only date celebrities. When I'm dating someone famous, I can find out anything about them: where they were the night before, who they were with, what they were doing, who they were dating before me. They can't hide. There are no secrets.

What's your one, no-fail technique to keep them coming back for more?

I'm a toe licker. And I'm great at phone sex. I look up sexy stories on the Internet and I read them like I'm coming up with them myself. Guys love that stuff. And they never know the truth.

What's a good way to initiate a threesome?

I think it's better with four. Really, two guys and a girl, or two girls and guy, those are odd numbers. It's easier to initiate a bigger group. My neighbor is a photographer. He has an after-hours party with all these models and dancers and whatever. They play strip blackjack. He puts on a porno. It always erupts into an orgy, always.

Aside from condoms and lube, what is the number one thing everyone should have in their sex drawer?

A whip. And restraints. And a ball for your mouth. Really, nothing's hotter. Keep them on hand, let your girlfriend find them; she'll know what to do.

JessiRae, 22

🦋 What can normal folks like us do to bed a model?

I've never actually dated a model, so let's think, what have guys done to get me in bed? Most just act like themselves, show me a good time, and are witty and charming. A few have tried to just spend money on me. Did it work? I'm not telling. My current boyfriend came across the bar to tell me that I was his dreamgirl: black hair with light eyes. The only problem was I have neither. He recovered somehow.

🦋 What's your one, no-fail technique to keep them coming back for more?

Most men like the way I do them when I'm on top. I don't just put it all in and rock back and forth. I kind of tease the tip, make them beg for me.

🦋 What's the worst faux pas someone can make in bed?

Making a big deal of sounds. Sex makes sounds. Don't make me feel uncomfortable about it, then expect me to feel sexy later.

🦋 Aside from condoms and lube, what is the number one thing everyone should have in their sex drawer?

Wet wipes. Especially if you've got a roommate. Who wants to run to the bathroom every time to clean up something a moistened tissue can do just as well?

🦋 Female ejaculation—ever experienced it? If so, how did you make it happen?

It happens from time to time. I have to be on top, though, then he moves my body back and forth, like he's sawing me across his cock. It hits something inside and I feel like I'm going to pee. You just have to relax and enjoy it.

🐱 A guy has gone limp and both parties feel inadequate. What can you do to alleviate the tension? How can you regain momentum?

The last time this happened to me, I told him that the greatest lay I'd ever had came from a guy who was too nervous to stay hard at first. That seemed to make him comfortable. Then I touched him all over, including places guys say they don't like to be touched. He was ready to go in no time. Of course, he was also ready to blow in no time, but what can you do?

Elisa, 21

Are there any poses/facial expressions people should avoid during sex? If so, what are they? And why should they be avoided?

Just try not to look like a killer at the moment of impact. I'd say 70 percent of the men I've been with make a face like they're killing an animal. It's horrifying. You've got to be really good to get invited back after that.

What's the proper answer when a lover asks how many partners you've had?

Six. It's not so many you're a whore, not so few you're a prude. You've just got to be sure you add one the next time he asks.

When is same-sex interaction just for fun and when does it mean you're bisexual?

In the case of girls, if you're doing it in front of a crowd, there's nothing gay about it. That's just looking for attention. Even behind closed doors, I'd say for most girls it's just experimenting. I've never done it, but I don't see any reason not to. Life is short. I'd like to say the same thing about guys, but it's different.

Aside from condoms and lube, what is the number one thing everyone should have in their sex drawer?

A vibrator. Men have good days and bad. My vibrator never once had to make up an excuse.

Do's and don'ts for dirty talking?

Make sure it's something your partner is comfortable with. Don't go around slapping asses and calling her names if she wants to be made love to. Of course, not everyone wants to be made love to every time.

Laura Lee, 21

🐚 **What should be known about bringing a camera into the bedroom?**

Lighting is hard. The only thing I would advise, if you're younger, is that you hide your tape very well. My mom found my tape. I have a funny dysfunctional family, though. All she said was that he had a little dick.

🐚 **Are there any poses/facial expressions people should avoid during sex?**

Smiling is weird. Just think about it, can you imagine someone grinning while they're on top of you? Don't do that. Really.

🐚 **My girlfriend always wants me to go down on her. I hate doing it, but I want to please her. Is there anything I can do to make it more enjoyable for me?**

Think of ice cream. Just think of it. If you've got a good imagination, I'll bet you'll be able to taste it, too.

🐚 **A guy has gone limp and both parties feel inadequate. How can you regain momentum?**

If it were to happen, and I'm not saying it has, but if it happened, and drugs weren't involved, I would recommend tying him up. I find once most guys are forced to give up control, they get turned on. If that still doesn't work, it's time to give up.

🐚 **My girlfriend is afraid of anal sex. How can I convince her?**

I told my boy I'd do it if he would. I stuck a vibrator in his ass and I never heard about it again. But if he'd still wanted it after that, I would've been down.

FORMER CATHOLIC SCHOOL STUDENTS

Liz, 24

What's the best way to suggest introducing a third partner into a new relationship?
"It worked for the Father, Son, and Holy Ghost."

Do open relationships ever work?
They work when both people are getting an equal amount of outside-the-relationship ass.

What's a mortal sin in the bedroom?
Unsolicited attempts at rear entry.

I'm all about ritual—candles, Enigma playing in the background, vanilla incense on occasion. Does any of this really matter if the sex is top-notch?
Not at all. If you're focused on tradition, you might lose sight of why you're there and what you're doing in the first place—something the Catholic Church can relate to.

Meghan, 24

🍂 Should I tell my current partner about my wild past?

This one works like trickle-down economics: you slowly reveal things over a long period of time. It's elementary. After a guy knows that shit is his, then he won't stress knowing that you were number 2,398 on Gene Simmons's hit list and once went down on a midget.

🍂 Rumor is, former Catholic school students are a sexed-up lot. What's with the myth?

Catholic school students are sexually repressed during their formative years, so when they get out into the real world they think they are in a constant porno.

🍂 How do I get over any reservations about rear entry?

Have some Anal-Eze on hand. That stuff is a magical potion. It will make you feel like a trained adult professional. Not that I've tried it or anything.

🍂 I've heard that Catholic girls give excellent head. Any tips?

It could be that we're just good on our knees. Do I owe it to my Catholic School roots? I think I just owe it to Phoebe Cates in *Fast Times at Ridgemont High.* My only tip is to make it look like it tastes like the most decadent chocolate devil's food cake dripping with creamy vanilla ice cream you've ever had the privilege to taste, and pretend that having it go down your throat isn't painful. In fact, the deeper it goes, the harder you should moan, because it counteracts the gagging reflex.

🍂 What's the most valuable sexual lesson you learned in Catholic school?

To disregard just about everything I learned about sex in Catholic school. I guess the most valuable is that most devout Catholics have eight to twelve children and can barely afford toothpaste for their small alcoholic armies.

Stephen, 24

🔥 **I'm interested in investigating hot role-play scenarios for beginners. Has the Catholic school uniform worked for you?**
Indeed, once I was sleeping in the English room during lunch. This girl I had a crush on found me all alone. I woke up and saw her standing there wearing a short plaid shirt and white knee-high leggings. She wanted me to come outside and play Frisbee, but I had a better idea. We had crazy sex right there in the classroom. The schoolgirl uniform is still my favorite.

🔥 **Rumor is, former Catholic school students are a sexed-up lot. What's with the myth?**
It seems to be true. I spent most of school thinking about the girls I had fucked or wanted to fuck. There was a math class where I had been with five of the girls in it. I used to sit there and wonder if any of them knew about the others. I failed math that year.

🔥 **As far as you're concerned, what's a mortal sin in the bedroom?**
The excessive use of teeth during oral sex.

🔥 **I've met someone with strong religious convictions and I'm worried that these convictions may follow us into bed. Should I be concerned or just play it by ear?**
There was a long time where I wanted to become a priest. I had already had tons of sex and done all the partying there was to do, so I thought that a life of service might be more fulfilling. My parents sent me to a Catholic university in Los Angeles. I soon found out religious convictions are null and void after dark in L.A. So I would play it by ear.

Sex Advice From

GAMERS

Gene, 28

I need to break up with a very nice gentleman because, aside from all his good qualities, I'm repelled by the natural scent of his body. He doesn't have BO; I just can't stand his musk.

Don't tell him. It could be very hurtful. I would say, "It's just not working out" rather than "You stink." If he has really bad BO you could suggest taking baths together, a nice shower maybe, but I wouldn't tell someone they stink. That's probably a little too honest.

What makes a video game sexy? Does that mean it turns you on?

In *God of War* there's a scene where two naked women are on the bed and you have sex with them and if you hit the buttons and the right key the bed starts rocking and a vase falls off the wall. I guess that's sexy. I mean, they put a lot of big-breasted, half-dressed women in most of the games. It's not really hot. It's more funny than anything—the moans of ecstasy in the background are hilarious.

What is a video game fetish that easily translates into sex play?

Hand-eye coordination. Being good at pushing buttons.

If your genitalia were a game controller, what would be the code to get you off?

I don't know. That's a good one. You definitely have to jiggle the joystick, and then it's a specific combination between the joystick and then pushing the right two buttons. Like circle, circle, x squared, joystick, circle.

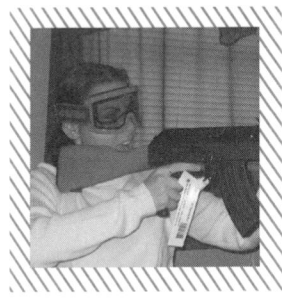

Narcissa, 18

🐱 **Aside from condoms and lube, what should everyone have in their sex arsenal?**
Fuzzy handcuffs, chocolate, and costumes are a must. Helllllllllllooooooooooo Nurse!

🐱 **How are gamers more likely to have an active fantasy life?**
I'd like to quote *Revenge of the Nerds* here: "All that jocks think about is sports; all nerds think about is sex." Of course gamers have more exciting fantasies. What do you think they're doing all alone in their basement room? Fraggin' away all night? I don't think so. Their devious minds are always plotting something.

🐱 **What video game equipment easily lends itself to sex play?**
A DualShock PS2 controller could be a functional little toy.

🐱 **What are good ways to tangle sex and video games?**
Shouting out radio commands (if you're an FPS addict) could be interesting. Fire in the hole!

🐱 **If your genitalia were a game controller, what would be the code to get you off?**
On a controller: up up down down up up down down.

ProperMethodz, 26

🎮 **Recently, it's taken me a long time to come to orgasm masturbating. I'm dating—but I find myself feeling tentative about getting hot and heavy with someone because I know they'll have to really put in some time before I get off. Isn't that asking a lot in the beginning?**

No way. If two people get together and want to have a good time then they know that there will be some concessions both will have to make. The beginning of any relationship is always a little clumsy. The fun part is figuring out what makes the other person tick. Regardless of the circumstance, I need to know the woman I'm with is getting her share for me to even get it up. If she's not enjoying herself I'll have a difficult time enjoying myself.

🎮 **What is a move a video game character can do that you wish you could use in sex?**

I'm sure it's in a game somewhere. I wish I had gills to breathe so that my nose wasn't blocked when I was going down on a woman.

🎮 **What is a video game fetish that easily translates into sex play?**

Tea bagging. It's when a player kills another and stands over them repeating the crouch move, which looks like you are tea bagging the person on the ground.

GUITAR SHOP EMPLOYEES

John, 37

How do your skills as a drummer apply to the bedroom?
Well, if you practice your paradiddles, once you get the basic rhythm down, there's also a certain rhythm that you and your mate will have. A little slow, a little fast.

What drummer is your sexual role model, and what could we learn from him?
Tommy Lee. Oh my goodness, what is there not to learn from Tommy Lee? Basically, he knows how to score backstage.

Is there a type of music, frequency, or sound that enables female orgasm?
Barry White had it pinned down, guys like him and Luther Vandross. Death metal, jazz, just doesn't work. For some reason Barry White and those guys really hit on something—the frequencies of their voice will lend to them actually writing in certain keys that are sexy, G major 7th, anything flat. Oh, and tempo. Tempo is very important.

Who do you think is hot that other people don't think is hot?
I like sort of heavyset women, cuz when wintertime comes, a big woman will help keep me warm. I'm a small guy!

Helen Gurley Brown, of *Cosmo,* has some excellent blow job tips. Do you have any insight into the matter?
I don't want to be nasty mouth, but—I like my balls licked. I just like them licked, and touched. That feels good!

Nell, 22

🐱 **My roommate fucks her boyfriend loudly at all hours of the night. It keeps me awake.**

Make her a mix tape of loud music and be like, "Hey, this is great sex music, I'm sure you'd enjoy it!" Or be like, "Hey, you know what they sell at this music store? They sell Auralex Foam! It's acoustic sound proofing."

🐱 **How many orgasms have you been responsible for in one evening?**

Well, probably four or five, but there were also toys involved, vibrators. I'm a lesbian, so it's with girls. It has to do with touching the entire body, and toys. I use the Water Dancer—it's a small body massager type thing.

🐱 **How do you let somebody down easy?**

"Oh, I'm sorry. I'm gay."

🐱 **What guitarist do you consider to be a sexual role model?**

I enjoy the guitar stylings of Tony Iommi of Black Sabbath. He makes do very well with what he has—he's missing fingers! He plays sexy chords, powerful, intense.

🐱 **What music have you had sex to, and enjoyed?**

It's painfully obvious just from looking at me—Tones on Tail's album *Night Music*. It's a great record to make loooove to.

🐱 **Any tips on how to make condom use more enjoyable?**

Market it to be some forbidden kinky thing you're not supposed to use, reverse psychology. Guys used to jerk off into condoms as some taboo thing, and that was more appealing than the idea of safe sex.

John, 36

What's the biggest mistake you've made in the sack?
Passing out.

Who do you think is hot that most people don't think is hot?
The columnist for the *Times,* Maureen Dowd. Something about her intellect says she'd be really good in the sack.

Do you have any tips for aspiring groupies?
Don't go after the keyboard player. We have too much to do at the end of the night.

Do you get offended when a girl spits?
Secret spitters are gross—I like to know when it happens, just in case she puts it on your roommate's shoes or something! They should find a good place for it, an appropriate place.

What's the most underrated fetish?
Most fetishes are overrated cuz they get in the way of actually messing around with skin. It's too much effort, especially when you drink as much as I do.

Sex Advice From

HAIRSTYLISTS

James, 32

🔥 **A hot chick washes hair at the salon I go to; is it weird to ask her out while she's washing my hair?**
Um, it's not weird, but I don't think you'll get a good response.

🔥 **If I'm a gay man, how can I tell if my stylish male hairdresser is gay without being uncouth?**
Ask direct questions: "Are you single?" "Are you married?" "Do you live by yourself?" I do that all the time with clients.

🔥 **How can I revamp my prudish image without looking cheap?**
Get a fantastic haircut and a pair of high heels. You don't have to wear a miniskirt, just tight jeans, high heels, great haircut.

🔥 **What's the best way to get a hairdresser to go home with you?**
Flirt. When you're sitting in the chair, where you put your hands while they're cutting can be very, very flirtatious.

🔥 **How so? What's the best hand position?**
Well, if your arms are on the edges of the rests, and the hairdresser is kind of leaning into the chair while cutting your hair, a lot of times there's an interaction, a sort of energy, and there's ways of communicating that.

Wendy, 29

🐚 **Should people get fancy with their pubic hair, i.e., use hair products? How far is too far?**

I feel like if it's done properly, you're not going to look at it and notice the "hairdo." And when it gets to the point where it actually becomes a hairdo, it just becomes a complete turnoff and it's really tacky.

🐚 **My boyfriend is beautiful but his foot-long ponytail is not. He would be so much cuter if he just chopped it off. If I can't fall in love with that ponytail does that mean we're doomed?**

Yes, you're doomed. But I would recommend cutting it off while he's asleep. Pretend it just came off on its own.

🐚 **How can you tell your significant other that they do something in everyday life that repulses you sexually? (For example: I would rather spoon-feed my boyfriend for the rest of our lives than continue to watch him eat noodle soup or spaghetti with his fingers.)**

I usually just come right out with it, just say it, "That's really grossing me out, you need to stop doing it or I can't see you anymore."

Heather, 29

How important is hair care below the belt? What's the proper amount of maintenance?

It's very important to have a nice trimmed pubic area. I don't know how attractive gray in the pubic area is. You could dye it, probably with something that is gentle, maybe Just for Men [a facial hair dye] or something like that. And you know, it doesn't have to be "just for men," necessarily.

My boyfriend is beautiful but his foot-long ponytail is not. He would be so much cuter if he just chopped it off. If I can't fall in love with that ponytail, does that mean we're doomed?

No. You don't have to keep it to yourself. You can say how you feel; you can say, "I think you would be so hot without the ponytail that I would want to have sex with you every day."

What's the best way to get a hairdresser to go home with you?

"My grandma is really sick and can't leave the house. Please come over and give her a haircut."

Aneesa, 29

How important is hair care below the belt? What's the proper amount of maintenance?
For girls, Brazilian waxes. For guys, just clean it up a little.

What's the best way to incorporate hair into sex?
Wigs.

A friend of mine just started hooking up with another friend. They are keeping it casual, which delights him; he is so impressed by her ability to keep their friendship and sex separate. The only problem is, she isn't doing that. She's confided in me that she's falling for him. I don't want to be the bearer of bad news for her—or make him freak out—but I feel I have to do something before this gets ugly. What should that something be?
I would tell the guy to tell the girl, "I like how casual this is," instead of having her start to spill her feelings. That seems like it would be the easier way.

What's the best way to get a hairdresser to go home with you?
If you're in the salon, offer to take them out to dinner, because they're going to be hungry after work. I mean, you've just sat there and talked for an hour, so you can usually tell if they're going to say no.

Carissa, 21

🦋 **How important is hair care below the belt? What's the proper amount of maintenance?**

If you're a woman, I'd recommend you wax. I myself like to leave a little landing strip just because I feel like a child if it's all gone.

🦋 **A hot chick washes hair at the salon I go to; is it weird to ask her out while she's washing my hair?**

I'm an assistant at my salon right now. I do a lot of hair washing and I would feel weird about that. I think the best way to go about that is to write your phone number on their tip envelope. That would be a sly way to do it, leave an enormous tip and your phone number.

🦋 **What's something everyone should have in their sex drawer other than condoms or lube?**

I like massage oils; those are always nice. I guess toys are always fun too. I hate to say it but I've never really invested in sexual toys, but I'd like to and I know that's a part of a lot of people's drawers. I also have boxes of lingerie.

INTERIOR
DESIGNERS

Maxwell, 39

I want to turn my bedroom into the perfect location for making a sex tape. What tips do you have on lighting?
You don't need natural light. You want a number of points of light. Forget the overhead light. You wanna have two lamps, one on either side of the bed, and at least a third. Make sure all the lighting is indirect—so you never see a bulb. So even if you have track lighting, you want to make sure the light hits the wall. You definitely want low lighting.

I love my vibrators, but let's face it, they're pretty tacky looking. Who makes the best design?
I think that the egg designs are really pretty. The Japanese mini designs are pretty attractive.

What are the best interiors for sex in public?
I really like the changing rooms at Banana Republic. They're really plush and they have full closing doors, and they're very carpeted. They're trying to be very stylish and they're easy to get in and out of. In New York, they're actually the biggest interior spaces you run into. And they leave you alone. At the more high-end stores, they never leave you alone. You can't escape.

What's the best piece of furniture to have sex on?
A really nice rug. Or a desk in an office.

What do you suggest to remove come stains?
There's nothing you can do. Get used to throwing things away.

Saana, 34

🐱 **I love my sex sling but it clashes with the room. Any thoughts?**

You can always reupholster it. Try a nice durable and washable fabric, like ballistic nylon. Or you could take your chair to an upholsterer and use it as a pattern, so you can have them remake it in almost any color. Depending on your interior, you could have a project of embroidering your sex chair or screen printing on it. That's a little bit of a hippy-dippy look, so it really depends on what you're going after.

🐱 **Likewise, I love my vibrators, but let's face it, they're pretty tacky looking. Who makes the best design?**

Betty Dodson's Barbell is made of stainless steel and uses PC muscle exercises. It's fabulous looking and would go with any decor.

🐱 **What can I do to dress up a hotel (or motel) room to make it a little more inviting?**

The lighting is usually really terrible. Just toss an old T-shirt over the lamp. That adds a nice quickie vibe.

🐱 **I think of my body as a house of love. Do you think I'm better off with a rug by the hearth or should I go bare?**

From a design standpoint, an appropriately scaled rug that is not too shaggy is the way to go. Think low pile.

Regina, 40

How do I turn my bedroom into the perfect location for making a sex tape?

If you want your space to look like a real porn set, get the cheapest stuff possible. Go to the Home Depot and get some of those cone lights with the clamp, and clamp them somewhere they won't be seen on camera, get some colored saran wrap; that works as a good gel. You might want to choose not to have a bed-spread, and not too many pillows. Try a fitted sheet with a high thread count. Sateen is nice; it's very smooth. Pillows are a good prop. A scarf over the lamp shade makes for some nice inexpensive mood lighting. Other props? Ice cubes, lube. Don't let the dog in. Unless you're into that.

What's the best piece of furniture to have sex on?

If you like it doggy style, I recommend a wing chair.

What do you suggest to remove come stains?

Most basic household detergents will remove come stains. It dries clear and has low acidity, and doesn't often stain. Blood stains are best removed if you use cold water immediately. For more stubborn stains, use a little bit of detergent, rubbed in with cold water.

Any tips for giving a good hand job?

In my opinion, giving a man a hand job is like saying you believe in blue balls. Don't do it.

Sex Advice From

LIFEGUARDS

Claude, 28

What sort of attitude should one take to lure a summer love?
This beach has its own little personality. If a girl comes down here and she's single, it's 'cause she's looking for a guy. You're not here because you want a nice quiet day at the beach; you're here because you want to get picked up. To come down here and have just one girl is really really difficult.

Should head always be returned?
No, not with me anyway. Most of the girls I've been with just suck at giving head anyway. Some girls have a really great body, so it's really great to go down on them. But for myself I don't even ask, I've been so disappointed in the past.

Is getting it on on the beach or under water overrated?
Yeah, it's kind of overrated. It takes away from the sensitivity of it. The shower is good, but submerged, it's no good.

What about having sex on the first date? How does that affect the longevity of the relationship?
I'd say second date. I usually don't pass the second date if things don't start to develop; it's not worth it. Most of the time that's why I'm going out on dates, to get laid. There's so many hot girls down here, it's not like you even have time to get to know their personality. To me, sex is very important in a relationship; if that stinks, I don't even want to go any further.

Judy, 23

🐱 Should head always be returned?
I think it's the polite thing to do, but you don't always have to be polite.

🐱 It's the first time you're hooking up with a guy and he slips a finger up your ass, is that okay?
Umm, yeah.

🐱 What's cheating? Is simultaneous masturbation cheating?
Yeah, that would be cheating.

🐱 Making out?
Yeah.

🐱 Flirting?
That's crossing the line.

🐱 Getting a phone number?
Yeah, cheating. Well, I don't know if that's cheating, but I'd be like you're going to cheat on me.

🐱 Is getting cheated on usually reason enough to break up?
Yeah. Once a cheater, always a cheater.

🐱 How about sex on the first date? How does it affect the longevity of a relationship?
I think for girls it doesn't, because we don't think, "I'm not going to want a relationship with him if I sleep with him the first night." But I think guys will view you differently if you do.

Gladstone, 24

What kind of fun can you have with lifeguarding equipment? Any good tricks?

The lifeguard shower is the greatest part, but the stands are great. I've been with a girl in the stands and it's a good time! You have to wait till nighttime for all that though.

What's the best way to start a naked dance party?

You charge people less to get in the less clothing they wear.

Is simultaneous masturbation cheating?

Oh, hell, no. I'm not touching her, she's not touching me.

Sex Advice From

MALE MODELS

Sebastian, 20

What's the proper answer when a lover asks how many partners you've had?

You shouldn't say, "None of your business," because they'll think you're a complete slut. I say, "I've had three relationships." Don't tell them about the one-night stands until you're firmly established. Then tell them if you want to show off. In the meantime, talking about relationships instead of sex makes you look like a gentleman.

Same-sex interaction: what's the line between "just for fun" and bisexual?

Even if a gay guy fucks a girl—which goes on all the time—he's still gay; he was just doing it for fun. But if he eats her pussy, he's bisexual. That's the line. You can't put the private part in your mouth. It works the other way too: two guys or two girls making out is just that, until someone puts something in their mouth.

Any advice on sex in public, from personal experience?

Would you count a bathroom? I know it doesn't sound public, but what if it was in the Metropolitan Museum of Art? Or Six Flags? Or the Barnes & Noble in Staten Island? It was all with one person; don't get the wrong idea. He'd just lean over and whisper a dirty fantasy about where we were at that very moment, and I'd get so turned on. A tip: bring lube, everywhere.

What's the worst faux pas someone can make in bed?

You've got to be verbal, but if it's going to cross over into some kind of role-play, you've got to warn your partner first. Don't start talking in a baby voice or pretend to be their daddy if they don't see it coming.

Rob, 29

Same-sex interaction: what's the line between "just for fun" and bisexual? Ever done it?
If they're still there for breakfast, you're bisexual. As far as having done it, who doesn't enjoy breakfast in bed occasionally?

What's the worst faux pas someone can make in bed?
Talking about their ex. You'd be surprised how many women have told me I'm better than their last. Yeah, it's a compliment, but what's the point?

Aside from condoms and lube, what is the number one thing everyone should have in their sex drawer?
A cock ring, preferably leather. Enhances, prolongs, intensifies.

Female ejaculation—ever experienced it? If so, how did you make it happen?
Squirters? I think that's only in the movies. I've had friends in "the industry." Those girls load up with water, then, uh, expel it for the camera.

What's the key to great cunnilingus?
Don't do it right after she's taken a shower. Wait until the end of the day. Let it marinate. Otherwise it just tastes like a rubbery piece of skin. Where's the fun in that? Girls are afraid when their pussy tastes like pussy. I don't know why. Let's bust that myth right now.

A guy has gone limp; both parties feel inadequate. What can you do to alleviate the tension and regain momentum?

Tell her it's the medication you're taking. It's the only way. Otherwise she'll never believe she's not fat, ugly, or old.

Jim, 18

What's your one no-fail technique to keep them coming back for more?
The reach-around. No matter what else I'm doing, I've always got one hand on her sweet spot.

What's the worst faux pas someone can make in bed?
I picked up the phone once. I thought I was being funny. My girlfriend at the time didn't see it that way.

Aside from condoms and lube, what is the number one thing everyone should have in their sex drawer?
Massage oil. Nothing gets the ladies hotter than a nice, long slow massage. Don't worry too much about the shoulders; it's all about the hands and feet.

Any tips for bringing a camera into the bedroom?
Whatever you do, don't put it at the foot of the bed. I did that once. Basically we made a tape looking up our butts.

My girlfriend always wants me to go down on her. I hate doing it, but I want to please her. Is there anything I can do to make it more enjoyable for me?
Don't press your face into her too hard; it makes it hard to breathe. It's much more enjoyable if you can breathe easy, and girls don't like too much pressure there anyway.

Do's and don'ts for dirty talk?
Tell her what you're fantasizing about. Don't call her names. Only girls in movies want to hear that they're sluts. Treat her like a lady, just a dirty lady, that's all.

Chris, 26

What's a good way to initiate a threesome?

If you really want to get freaky, rent a hotel room, even if you're right around the corner from your house. Girls always do more than they ever thought they could or would in hotel rooms. It's like a fantasy world in there. They walk in and think, "This is so not my life." Then they're willing to go crazy.

What's your one no-fail technique to keep them coming back for more?

Most girls have never actually been kissed all over. I know it sounds cliché, but if you're the first one to kiss the insides of her elbows or the back side of her knees, she'll be yours forever.

Are there any facial expressions or poses that should be avoided during sex?

Most guys like it if a girl acts like she's either in pain or in ecstasy. Just about any face you can make fits into those two categories.

Any tips for bringing a camera into the bedroom?

Get a tripod first. It's so much dirtier in a strange, professional way.

Do's and don'ts for dirty talking?

Whisper. Shouting is for flashers; whispering is for perverts—the good kind.

MASSAGE THERAPISTS

Elizabeth, 33

🐱 **What's the most erotic nongenital pressure point?**
Earlobes. Give them a squeeze.

🐱 **Massage for seduction: what's the key? What areas should be touched or avoided? Is there a hand motion or pressure level that's key?**
Don't hurt them, work on hands and forearms so you can be face to face, and work along the face and ears. That can be sensual or nonsensual, depending on what you bring to it. And stay away from baby oil. That's frightening!

🐱 **Tips for shooting an amateur porn video?**
Focus more on what women want to see. Forget the chrome-dome, over-the-top shots, like those of the woman moaning in ecstasy just after he lays her down. They need to get away from that. Men need to work a little harder and do more foreplay.

Brittaney, 28

How can I suggest giving my date a massage without sounding sleazy?

Find out what your date does all day. If they stand on their feet all day, say, "Your feet look tired, can I rub them?" That shows you're listening to what the other person has to say and you're cognizant of their stresses. You don't want to make them uncomfortable. If you've been hiking together all day, you might not ask to massage their sweaty feet. Use common sense.

Is there a good massage oil that doesn't feel like you're smearing Crisco all over your partner?

I would go with a lotion rather than an oil, especially for a man massaging a woman. Lotion is emulsified, so it won't leave that greasy film in the person's hair. Oil stains clothes, too. Go to any natural food place and get an unscented, natural body lotion. Scents can send the wrong impression. Something too musky or voluptuous might make the person think you're a little fruity, or that you do this with everyone you invite over.

What's the best way to pick up a masseuse?

Don't say "masseuse," people will hate you for that. Say "massage therapist." The best way is don't be their client. Don't offer a massage either. We'll just be hypercritical of your technique.

Describe your no-fail, all-purpose orgasm-inducing move.

Man on top. I guess it's called "the Butterfly." It's like missionary position, but the woman wraps her legs around his legs and he's at a forty-five-degree angle. The key is pubic-to-pubic contact, like a grinding motion. That's for women, but I'm sure it does an equally good job for men.

Liam, 33

Massage for seduction: what's the key? What areas should be touched or avoided?

Hands and feet can be pretty erotic. So can the stomach and the inside of the thighs. You have to be careful working in those areas, though. Watch your pace.

Tips for shooting an amateur porn video?

Good lighting, and get the clutter out of the background. Any time I look at a personals ad, I always see these bad pictures of a bunch of shit in the background. Old furniture is an absolute turnoff.

Describe your no-fail, all-purpose orgasm-inducing move.

Anal penetration. It always works. There's something guarded about that area, but once you're able to let go of it, it releases something ferocious.

Sex Advice From

MENSA
MEMBERS

Kristin, 51

🐱 **What's the smartest thing anyone's ever done to you?**

A very close friend of mine has a foot fetish. I let him have his way with my feet. It was foot massage like I've never known before.

🐱 **What is the number one thing, other than condoms, that everyone should have in their sex drawer?**

Mango butter. You can use it for massage, you can use it for lube. It smells like mango. Semi-edible if you like mangoes. It's good for sensuous massage, touching.

🐱 **Dirty talk: should it be kept to one- and two-syllable words or do Mensa folk stick to SAT words?**

Dirty words should be short. It's not a good time to be intellectual; you're supposed to be on an instinctual level when you're having sex.

🐱 **What is the best BJ move?**

The tip of your tongue right underneath the little piece of skin behind the head, the frenum. Wiggle it back and forth. Don't take it into your month for a real long time. Just go up and down the shaft, go back to that spot and wiggle your tongue there.

Avram, 24

Who's better in bed, the brain or beauty?
The girls that aren't hot, they have to try a little bit harder. Because they are on some level or subconsciously competing with the hotter girls. They're freakier.

What's the dumbest thing you ever did during a sexual act?
When I started getting close to this new girl, I didn't masturbate for three weeks. The first time we hooked up it was three seconds and that's it. That was pretty dumb. Maybe take a couple days off but not three weeks. After I exploded in her mouth I was a little embarrassed. I guess she thought it was sort of flattering.

What's the smartest thing anyone's ever done to you?
One time, a girl bought me a lap dance.

What is the number one thing, other than condoms, that everyone should have in their sex drawer?
The number of a taxi service.

Best BJ move?

Number one: the mouth may be enough for some guys but for some of us we need a mouth and a hand or two. There's also circular motion—clockwise, counterclockwise. It's good to do forward and back, left and right. Work it like a joystick.

 Any tips for a successful hand job?

For hand jobs, I would say the shaft is more important than the head. It hurts too much if you go after the head. Again, you want side to side motion, some circular motion. When a girl uses her natural wetness for a hand job, that's hot too.

Paula, 26

🐚 Who's better in bed, the brain or beauty?

I would have to say the beauty is better in bed. The smartest guy I dated was boring in bed. The handsomest people I ever dated have definitely been the best. I think they had more confidence and they're able to take control a lot more. Smart guys grew up insecure about the way they look. Normally, they're not very athletic, which translates to not having a lot of stamina in the bedroom.

🐚 Do the contents of a person's bookshelf affect whether or not you want to have sex with them? Is there any book or magazine that you could find in a potential lover's home that would send you running?

Oh my God, this is so embarrassing! Here's a story: I dated a guy, in the first few weeks of dating him I opened up his dresser drawer to get a T-shirt, which he told me to do. As soon as he said, "Oh yeah, the third drawer!" he gasped. I opened the drawer and there was a *Barely Legal* video tape. Any interest in underage girls is not attractive at all.

🐚 What book would turn you on?

One of the lesser-known F. Scott Fitzgerald books like *This Side of Paradise* or *Tender Is the Night*. I'm not into books that are like the generic, cool book.

🐚 Number one rule for being a fuck buddy?

Always be available. If your only job is to supply sexual pleasure, you better be around when I need it.

Ian, 28

 Who's better in bed, the brain or beauty?
Up until they're twenty or twenty-one, the prettier people have more experience so they're going to be better to sleep with. As you get older, everything starts evening out.

 What is the best BJ move?
The spontaneous blow job. Depending on your mood that could be the perfect thing. Maybe while you're doing something else, like a crossword puzzle. I would think, "Yeah, I can do those two things at the same time."

 Any tips for a successful hand job?
Do it in the shower. And don't wear rings! Some people don't realize that they have them on.

MIDWIVES

Janna, 29

🐚 **What's the most effective way to deal with a partner who is at the emotional mercy of her hormones?**
Telling her that she's beautiful all the time and just generally being thoughtful and sweet, just being understanding and giving a lot of praise—but it should be done with sincerity.

🐚 **What lube is most like the real thing?**
There's certainly the silicone ones. KY is kind of goopy. Astroglide is all right. The flavored, scented ones, you just want to be careful about what's in it. The sugar can give you an infection.

🐚 **I'm afraid that having children will stretch out my vagina. What can I do about it?**
Kegel exercises. They even have different barbells and different things you can use to improve your pelvic floor tone, and it will not only improve your sex life but it will make you less likely to pee on yourself when you cough or laugh. That happens to a lot of women but no one talks about it.

Holly, 49

I'm trying to get pregnant. What's the best position for me to do it in?

The position you lay in after lovemaking is more important than the position you're in when he ejaculates. It's a good idea to stay down after sex and at that point you might want to have your hips elevated.

Is it appropriate to incorporate lactation into sex play? Are there any health considerations?

A lot of women find they enjoy having their breasts suckled, and breasts can become more for sexual enjoyment rather than just for nurturing their child. Breast milk is yummy, which is why babies love it. If you have a very small baby, you don't want the partner competing with the baby, but that is the only downside.

No matter how turned on I am, I just don't get that wet. Is there something wrong with me?

Well, nature is such a little trickster. You are the most lubricated and the most horny when you are the most fertile. Near ovulation is when you are wettest and then there are other times during the cycle that you might be turned on but you just have that dry white mucus so you are not going to be that lusciously wet.

What should you never say to a midwife who you want to date? What's the biggest turnoff?

I don't really appreciate if somebody sees a midwife as a combination of prostitute, surrogate mom, sacred whore, that kind of thing.

Peggy, 56

🐱 **Any truth to old wives' tales that positions or frequency of sex can determine a baby's gender?**

Actually, there is some truth to the timing of intercourse affecting the gender. It has to do with the acidity of the vagina and the alkalinity of the vagina, and the thickness of the cervical mucous.

🐱 **What do you think about the idea that the G-spot is designed to help a woman feel a rush of pleasure during the last few moments of labor?**

Could be! Could be that everything is physiologically tied together in a certain way to make the whole process work. I've seen women have a mini-orgasm from breast-feeding, but I've never actually seen it at labor or birth.

🐱 **Got any good herbal remedies to rev up my sex life?**

Not in pregnancy! If you are pregnant, don't take the risk. For example, you can take cohosh to rev up your sex life when you're not pregnant, but when you are pregnant it can cause miscarriage and premature labor.

🐱 **What are some fun sexual positions a couple can try during the woman's last trimester of pregnancy?**

Comfort is key. If you can't get comfortable, you can't relax. If you can't relax, you can't get excited. A lot of women say, "Side lying is really working for me." Many women like hands and knees.

Devi, 25

🦋 I think I get too wet during sex. Do I have a medical problem?
There is a big controversy over the existence of the G-spot and whether G-spot orgasm and ejaculation occur. But, I think that women who think they are getting too wet are actually ejaculating; they just don't realize it.

🦋 I'm afraid that having children will stretch out my vagina. What can I do about it?
It is good to be proactive throughout the whole pregnancy. Midwives often recommend perineal massage. You can either do it yourself or with a partner. You use an oil, often almond oil, and slowly work on stretching that whole area out. Stretching before you give birth and keeping it toned doing Kegels will help avoid tears. You want to avoid tears because they can cause scar tissue, which is a lot harder to work with.

🦋 My boyfriend comes too fast. How can I make him last longer?
Unless you really love intercourse, premature ejaculation doesn't have to be seen as a problem. It's only a problem if you are only defining sex as penetrative sex. So, before you try to have intercourse you can try other things or you can have sex for a little bit then withdraw and tease each other and build up to it gradually. If penetration doesn't last long enough, you can then use a vibrator or a dildo. You can also work on breathing techniques. That's a lot of what Tantric sex is about, more focus on a full-body orgasm.

What should you never say to a midwife who you want to have sex with?

I think you would stir a few pots if you said, "I think elective cesareans are a great idea."

Sex Advice From

MUSIC CRITICS

Jessica, 29

What is the quickest way to turn on a music critic and why?
From the casual observation of my male peers, I would say if you are under twenty-three, like a little Xanax with your beer, and are heartened by being someone's plus-one and/or you find midlife crisis "sexy," your chances of scoring are in the 90 percent range.

As a gay male my penis is everything. The only problem is that it is bent at a right angle when erect. How can I warn men of my problem without scaring them away?
I would maybe make a T-shirt explaining the situation, either using iron-on letters, or if you are kind of punk—a sharpie. Roll up to the Manhole on a Friday night, and rock your "Bent Dick" shirt or whatever with confidence and pride. Chances are there is going to be some dude there who is trolling in hopes of finding a special penis like yours, and will be so relieved by how easy you made it for him to find you.

My wife has begun favoring her dildo over me. How can I compete with a dildo five times the size of my real thing?
Five times? What is she using, a drain auger?

I'm running out of effective pickup lines. I need one that'll get the ladies in one shot. Ideas?
I think that unless you're trolling on-campus Irish bars on ladies' night after finals, you are not likely to find a girl who'll cut as a result of a single, simple phrase. I would say go for honesty—a casual but not creepy expression along the lines of "I'd really like to fuck you" can go a long way. If that does not work, laugh at her jokes and compliment her hair a lot.

Kurt, a.k.a. DJ El Toro, 37

What makes a music critic a better lover?

A good music critic should be attuned to what their partner(s) are saying, either verbally or with body language, because we should be finely tuned to paying attention to subtlety. They should be open to trying new things, because staying ahead of trends is key to making a living in this business. They should be articulate about what they enjoy—you get paid to share your opinion, dumb ass. Know that it is never, ever acceptable to play This Mortal Coil, Roxy Music, or Spiritualized while having sex.

Recently I've realized I'm aroused by scat porn and want to try it with my girlfriend. However, I'm afraid if I tell my girlfriend she'll leave me. How can I satisfy my sexual curiosity for scat without jeopardizing my relationship?

I'd say start by trying to open up the discussion and playing to activities pitched somewhere between vanilla in-and-out and scat on the extremity scale—golden showers seem to be much less offensive to a lot of people—and see how it progresses from there. Or explore at your own peril on the Internet, and run the risk of getting dumped (no pun intended) when she checks what Web sites you've visited recently.

What is the most important sexual trick of the trade that you know?

Never be afraid to jam two fingers up someone's ass. If they don't like it—or they want something bigger up there right now—they'll let you know. I'm a big fan of making the most of your vocabulary and talking filthy, too. Tap into people's fantasies and then integrate what you're getting back from them. Being able to keep your mouth shut after the fact is pretty key, too.

Julianne, 29

What is the quickest way to turn on a music critic?
Play side C of LL Cool J's greatest hits (the slow jams) and don't go reciting liner-note minutiae when you're supposed to be kissing me.

What makes a music critic a better lover?
We're intelligent, eloquent, and we make terrific mix tapes. We have a superior understanding of rhythm and a select few of us are fabulous dancers, too.

Do all music critics fuck each other? If so, how does a guy like me get in on the music critic action?
Become a feminist. It may not work, but at least you'll be liberating yourself from the patriarchy that oppresses you.

My boyfriend really wants me to get kinky with him and surprise him with new stuff in bed. What do you suggest?
I would test the waters with a little light bondage, blindfolds, and Polaroids . . . you gotta ease into it before you start wrapping twine around his scrotum and wearing a plushy costume, you know?

Describe a new sexual position you highly recommend that you have created yourself.
This one I call the "Rhythm Nation 2005," inspired by my choreography idols Janet Jackson and Paula Abdul: do the snake onto your man and then like Mos Def said, just bounce.

How can I get off quicker? Help!
Finger in ass, honey. Finger. In. Ass.

Sex Advice From

NUDISTS

Ann, 25

🐱 **I love having guys go down on me, but I get insecure when they're all up close and personal. How can I get more comfortable with it?**

When you're completely alone, be naked. When you're not with your boyfriend, or friends, or at a dinner party, be naked. Once you're comfortable by yourself, then it'll work better in front of others.

🐱 **How can I make my partner more comfortable without gratuitous compliments?**

I'm a big fan of constant touching because I feel like if you have your hands on something, it makes it okay. Like, I've had partners who were maybe uncomfortable with their enormous amounts of chest hair, but once your run your hands on something and make it tactile it helps to defuse the self-consciousness.

🐱 **I'm a morning person, but my boy is a grumpy bitch. Can I reform him?**

Allow both yourself and your partner to brush your teeth. Another thing you can do, if you want it bad, is be aggressive. Just crawl on top, start kissing, and just put it in. Let them know you're going to do all the work.

🐱 **Have you ever made a sexual mistake that you would like to advise others against?**

I have, on an uncircumcised penis, pulled the skin down too far. He did not like that.

Elvin and Eric, both 25

How does being a nudist influence your sex life?

Elvin: I'm able to concentrate better and last longer.

How can I get more comfortable with myself naked?

Elvin: I spend about an hour in the morning in front of the mirror naked doing aerobics and stretching. Once you see yourself in athletic poses you learn to see your body and all its potential.

What is the nudist substitute for a strip tease?

Eric: Body butter and an erection.

Do nudists dress up to role-play?

Elvin: Maybe once or twice a year. Especially in the fall. My girlfriend likes it when I dress up as a teacher. A geeky teacher. It unleashes a new passion.

My guy is so sexy when he's girlish. I'd love for him to wear some panties and a skirt and a bra. What's the best way to introduce this?

Elvin: Get him alone and watch some videos of girl-on-girl action. Tell him how cute you think he is when he flips his hair, tell him that's what you like about him and tell him that's what turns you on.

Eric: Then get him hot and bothered, take him by the balls and tell him "You know what, I'm never going to get you off ever again unless you get into these panties."

What are the tricks to giving great oral sex?

Eric: Well, you know people are different. I like to ease into it, but some people like to be attacked. I personally like to go slow, fast, slow, circular, and, you know, don't be afraid to emphasize.

What is the sexiest part of the body that gets ignored during sex?

Elvin: Testicles.

Eric: Or hands and feet. Anything in the shadows, like behind the ears.

What's a sex mistake that you'd like to warn others against?

Elvin: Don't assume you know how to use a whip.

Jada, 25

🐱 **How does being a nudist influence and enhance your sex life?**

It makes everything less of a big deal. Doing all these nude activities, you start to distinguish nudity and sexuality. It's sort of like deconstructing sex a little more. Sex can just be an act, like it doesn't have to come with so much emotional baggage and personal baggage. It can just be a physical exchange if you choose to have it be that way.

🐱 **Biggest sexual mistake you ever made, and why you want to warn others against it as a public service?**

Well, there are so many. But they're all the common ones like trusting pulling out as a form of birth control. Things like that.

🐱 **What is the one thing no one should ever do when going down on a woman?**

Never, ever, ever say something like, "Doesn't smell so good" or "When was the last time you showered?" You never say anything that's going to give someone else a complex, because that's rude. They'll always be wondering how they smell or taste.

Paul, 43

How does being a nudist influence and enhance your sex life?

It doesn't always influence it positively because I have the desire to be totally nude whenever there's a sexual encounter. I don't like to do it with my boots on and that restricts the when and where I can do it. If I want to get it on in a taxi, I have to take it all off or else it feels cramped.

What is the segue into polyamory?

If you're interested in exploring it, there are a couple of really good books, mostly about radical honesty. You can go to lovingmore.com, get the book, and leave it on the coffee table. Say it was something you picked up on the Internet and you thought it'd be interesting and then go from there.

Sexiest ignored body part?

Armpits and that spot on your foot just before the heel where it's kind of ticklish. Sometimes I'll lick there and see what happens. If I get a good response, I'll stay there.

Sex mistake to warn others against?

Getting so drugged up, or being in such a situation that you can't communicate, you can't say, "Where are the condoms? Are we doing this safely? Do I know where my hand has been and where your mouth has been?"

Sex Advice From

OB/GYNs

Dr. Andrew Ditchik, 43

How exactly do you locate the legendary G-spot? And cause G-spot orgasm?

It's anterior, underneath the pubic bone, a roughened region. If you want to find it, reach up and back and reach for the ridged area. That seems to be the area that most women respond to.

Has a job that involves looking at vulvas affected your sex life?

Issues have come up with my girlfriend or with my ex-wife. They wonder, "Don't you get aroused by the women?" They are concerned because you look at this every day and wonder, "Could you still be interested in me?" Yes, I'm still interested in you. You're not on the table. You're not a patient.

What is the strangest question a patient has ever asked you?

Is it normal that every time that I take a shower my palms bleed?

Dr. Vanessa Cullins, 47

🐚 **Sometimes I feel unfresh down there. Douching, sprays, and powders are supposed to be unhealthy, right? What can I do?**

Daily bathing, and consider those little Huggies wipes they have for babies. You can carry those little towelettes in your purse and use them whenever you feel like you want to wipe the genitals.

🐚 **I'm not comfortable using my partner's sex toys because I know they've been used with other people. Should I insist on new ones?**

My preference is to get some new sex toys that are just sex toys for this particular union. Especially the penetrative sex toys. Bacteria and viruses don't live that long on inanimate surfaces, so technically soap and alcohol and water are okay if the toy isn't used immediately after a former partner has used it. But someone definitely needs new sex toys if she has it in the back of her mind that they are unclean or that they have been used by another woman.

🐚 **Any tips for pre-anal-sex hygiene? Do I really need to have an enema?**

Most people who have anal intercourse do not encounter a situation where you have a load of feces coming out unless the person is sick or incontinent. The most important thing from a woman's point of view is to never go from anal to vagina and from a man and a woman's point of view, never go from anal to oral. Don't be moving that bacteria around.

Many women can't seem to have an orgasm during vaginal sex unless a finger is employed. Is there anything they can do to change that?

The goal is how her clitoris can get direct stimulation. The woman-on-top position may be a way that she can maneuver so that she has direct stimulation of her clitoris without using his or her hand. She may be able to lean forward and be more up against his mons and the shaft of his penis as it relates to her clitoris. If she is wearing a thong and places the side of it up against her clitoris, then the motion of penetration may result in some direct stimulation.

Dr. Aren Gottlieb, 33

🐚 **Best way to tell a prospective partner I carry the herpes virus (but am currently outbreak free with medication)?**

There is no best way to tell someone, but you have to be honest. If you have an open relationship to begin with, then it really shouldn't be an awful thing to discuss.

🐚 **I'd like my girlfriend to start doing Kegels to strengthen her vaginal muscles. How do I tell her without sounding like an offensive boor?**

Is there a really good way? No. But you might want to say, "Well, I was sitting in the doctor's office waiting and I was reading in *Glamour* magazine that doing Kegel exercises can help you tighten your perineum and it can prevent you from having incontinence in the future." Something along those lines.

Dr. Sabria Ishoof, 31

What can I do to prevent catching HPV?

You can't. Any woman that is sexually active is going to have HPV exposure. Remember it's from genital contact, not just intercourse. It can live on your skin. It can live on your labia. On the penis. But even no sexual contact can pass the virus. In most people, it doesn't necessarily cause genital warts, so you don't know, but later on you can have abnormalities with your pap smear.

My penis is too big for several women I've been with. What can I do?

One of the things you can do is to put pillows under her bottom, which can tilt the pelvis up a little bit and allow a little bit more control. This is also good because you are not necessarily flat in an uncomfortable position where you can't control the extent to which penetration occurs. The thing that makes a woman uncomfortable is when the penis hits the cervix. The other thing is lubrication. Make sure that if there is not enough natural lubricant you use an artificial lube. I usually recommend Astroglide. It's not as drying as KY.

OLYMPIANS

Howard, 37, Badminton

What kind of training and dietary regimen helps you perform well in bed?

I just normally do my routine training, a lot of anaerobic stuff, doing sprints. For that situation, I'd do a lot hip abduction, the one where you sit on the chair and close and open your legs.

You're having sex with someone new, and you don't know if their endurance matches yours. How do you spend your energy? Is it better to be the sprinter or the marathon runner?

It's best if you have both worlds. Start off strong and finish strong.

What's the best way to pick up an Olympian?

Catch their attention, and start talking about what they do. "Hey, I saw you play yesterday."

I hear swimmers shave everything. What's the best way to convince that special someone to go hairless in that special place?

Tell her to watch a porno. Chicks like to watch them just as much as guys. Tell her, "Boy, she looks sexy bald."

Curt, 37, Track and Field

Is it true that Olympians like to get busy with each other at competitions, and is it considered unpatriotic to have sex with a competitor from another nation?

It's true, but probably not any more so than when young people are together in any situation. One of my favorite stats is how many condoms are used at each Olympic games, but I don't know if that's accurate, because they just throw six condoms into your bag. Unpatriotic? No, you'll be viewed as more of a goodwill ambassador.

Which of the Olympic sports sees the most action?

The sports that are over in the first week have the most opportunity to hook up and party. The premier sport that's over in the first week is swimming, and they live up to their reputation. Track and field doesn't start until the second week, so you have less partying and socializing time.

What do you have to do to score a perfect ten in bed?

Understand your partner's needs, whether what they want from the relationship is physical or mental. I like a partner who vocalizes what they need or desire.

Your partner has a big mirror on his or her closet. Is it narcissistic to pay attention to your own fine physique in the mirror during the act?

The mirror's there for a purpose, isn't it? The trick is when she asks what you're looking at you might not want to say it's you. Say it's her.

What's the best way to pick up an Olympian?

It matters if you're a man or woman. Male Olympians, like men in general, are a lot easier to pick up. But be physically fit yourself. For me, that's the number one turn-on. Flirting wise, if you're into their sport, that will help a lot.

Omar, 30, Water Polo

Is it true that Olympians like to get busy with each other at competitions, and is it considered unpatriotic to have sex with a competitor from another nation?

Athletes in general are horny bastards. But at the Olympics, there's so much pressure and everyone is so stressed out that it's not happening. Once they finish competing, then it turns into this huge orgy. When you go outside the country, America is the country everyone loves to hate and hates to love. Initially, they give you no love, but when no one is looking they give you lots of love. Know what I'm saying?

Which of the Olympic sports sees the most action?

The water polo guys do well. Basketball guys definitely do well. Swimmers definitely get the most action.

You're in an established sexual relationship. How do you introduce a friend to the team?

Start out slow. Start watching a little porn or reading magazines together so it's okay looking at other people. Once you've done that, ask joking questions like, "Would you ever kiss another girl?" If they say yes, you're like, "Damn, how about going to the strip club with me?" Then ask, "Would you ever consider bringing another girl in?" It's like baby steps.

What's the best way to pick up an Olympian?

For me it's easy—you just have to be pretty. The problem is that a lot of Olympians have big heads, so if you haven't done something great already, it's hard to get their eye. And almost everybody ends up marrying someone they trained with.

Genai, 28, Water Polo

How do you express your competitive instinct between the sheets?
That's one time I'm trying to lose. I'm always trying to come in last.

Which of the Olympic sports sees the most action?
Water polo has a reputation, and that's not even including myself.

What do you have to do to score a perfect ten in bed?
Like Eddie Murphy said, once you've made a girl say, "Ohhh, ohhhh," you can ask for anything you want.

Sexually speaking, what's the most important muscle, and why is it so special?
I'd say your abs, because your abs move your hips.

You're in an established sexual relationship. How do you introduce a friend to the team?
That's a tough one. If you have a serious girlfriend, you can't. If you find out, let me know.

What's the best way to pick up an Olympian?
Show interest—you don't necessarily need to even know anything about the sport.

Sex Advice From

OPERA SINGERS

Becca, 25

💋 **Best opera to listen to for tender lovemaking?**
La Boheme would be a good choice.

💋 **Hard-core fucking?**
Pagliacci. That's all about fucking.

💋 **The opera is?**
Well, the two lovers—Nedda and Silvio—sing this duet, and it's just about fucking.

💋 **How can I learn to deep throat?**
You have to use a lot of willpower. You just have to completely lower your larynx and breathe through your nose. And just take it.

💋 **What does every man want more of in bed, other than oral sex?**
Anal sex!

💋 **What does every woman want more of, other than oral sex?**
More rough sex.

💋 **Do you think guys are naturally a little inhibited?**
Yeah. They think they're gonna break you, when really they should just kinda grab you and throw you around.

💋 **What's the best nontraditional sex toy?**
I would say a hairbrush. You can use the bristly part for clitoral stimulation, and the handle for penetration.

Molly, 23

🐱 Best opera to listen to for tender lovemaking?
Something very easy to listen to. Either Mozart or maybe Puccini.

🐱 Hard-core fucking?
Carmen, "L'Amour"! But I think something not opera might be better—Beethoven or Stravinsky, something passionate.

🐱 How can I learn to deep throat?
You have your soft palate and your hard palate, and you raise up your soft palate, in the back, and you can open your mouth up a lot wider.

🐱 What's the best nontraditional sex toy?
The pillow.

🐱 What's the best position for mutual quick orgasm?
Guy sitting in a chair, and girl on top, straddling.

When you come on someone's face, should you just do it or ask first?

I think you need to ask. If you are a guy, and a girl is coming, that's fine, that's cool. But if you're a girl . . . I guess it depends on the kind of relationship you're in. If it's someone you haven't been seeing seriously, you should find a way of announcing what you're doing without breaking the mood.

Is Webcamming (masturbating while looking at someone on a Webcam and chatting) cheating?

I'd be pissed, but obviously they're unhappy with their sex life if they're doing shit like that, you know.

Quincy, 25

What are some sex techniques I could learn from a trained opera singer?

Sex is a lot like performing a leading opera role. The most important thing that a singer has to remember when performing a large role is not to blow their load too early. The singer should remember to pace himself and not exhaust all of his energy before the final scene. This applies to having good sex, too. If you know you can't go that long with her on top before you come, don't start off with her on top—leave that for last.

How can I learn to deep throat?

Ladies, if you're having problems, I can tell you that 99 percent of your problem is tongue tension. The most common reaction of women is to pull their tongue down, and back, to try and create more space. What actually happens when you do this, though, is you create unnecessary tension in the middle of your tongue. Open your mouth just wide enough for his cock to fit but don't open too wide, you don't want to create jaw tension. Make sure the tip of your tongue rests comfortably in a relaxed way against your bottom front teeth. If you keep this position you should be able to take in as much dick as he has to offer. Oh, and don't try to suck on his dick as it's going in, only create suction when it's being pulled out.

I think my girlfriend is faking her orgasms. How can I tell?

Just give her my little test. When she starts to get all noisy and shit like she's about to come, just politely pull your dick out before she reaches her peak, and if she gets mad and begs you to put it back in, well, ha, my dear friend, she was not faking it. But if when you pull it out, she just lies down and is like, "Baby, that was great," well, she's a fraud.

Josh, 24

Best opera to listen to for tender lovemaking?

Something from the romantic composers would be nice. Maybe Verdi's *Aida*. I love the "Liebestod" from *Tristan und Isolde,* but a lot of other things from Wagner might not be so gentle.

Hard-core fucking?

Something from the twenty-first century would be a good place to find opera that is unpredictable or harsh. I mean, it exists in older works, but I think Stravinsky might be a good place to start. His ballets would be perfect.

What does every man want more of?

More frequency! Every man wants to have it more often.

What does every woman want more of?

Women want more affection after sex.

What's the best nontraditional sex toy?

Fresh fruit.

I think my girlfriend is faking her orgasms. How can I tell?

Use a vibrator on her, and compare the way she reacts to you at your best, to the way she reacts with the vibrator. You should be able to figure it out. But chances are . . . she's faking it.

Sex Advice From

ORGANIC FARMERS

Matthew, 40

What can animals teach us about the right way to have sex?
Don't limit it to one partner.

I'm interested in a girl I work with. How can I let her know without crossing the line into sexual harassment?
I'd say, "Let's go out for coffee," or whatever people are drinking these days. Then just see what happens. Just make sure there are two chairs, so she doesn't have to sit on your lap.

What's the best way to convince your partner to have anal sex with you?
In my opinion, I don't think that has anything to do with love. I think at that point, you'd almost be saying to the person, "I don't love you." [*Laughs.*] I hope I'm not coming off as a prude. Other people might say, "I'm in love, so flip it over." I guess I'm making it obvious I've never done, or requested, the Charlemagne.

You call anal sex "the Charlemagne"?
Yeah. And if you want, on your Web site you can start calling it "the Charlemagne."

Brooke, 32

🐛 **Where's the best place on the farm for a roll in the hay?**
The big long grass in the back. Just not the hay. Hay is itchy and gets in the wrong places.

🐛 **Is there a place for fresh produce in your sexual toy chest?**
Oh yeah, of course. That would be zucchini.

🐛 **What can animals teach us about the right way to have sex?**
Faster is better sometimes.

🐛 **What do you wear when you're looking to hook up with someone on the farm?**
No makeup. There's something about no makeup and a ponytail that just gets everybody going.

🐛 **What's the most common oral sex mistake men make? Women?**
Men stay too long on the same spot. You need to move around. You need variety in momentum and in area. As far as women on men, I don't think there are any. I've never gotten a complaint, so I don't know.

Steve, 35

Is there a place for fresh produce among your sexual toy chest?

Always. Especially strawberries and oranges.

What can animals teach us about the right way to have sex?

Do it often, and use your instinct!

Pigs orgasm for thirty minutes. What can human beings do to feel less inadequate?

Have more sex. Make it up with quantity.

PERFORMANCE ARTISTS

Tanya, a.k.a. Tanya O'Debra, 25

🐱 How long should sex last?

The penis-in-vagina part should only be twenty minutes, tops. No more than that.

🐱 What tips would you give non-performers who want to woo a lover by singing or stripping or dancing, etc.?

Be original. If you're the guy, maybe you should be a naughty nurse—some sort of reversal. Do something different.

🐱 Under what circumstances is it okay to sleep your way to fame and fortune?

If everybody's really cute, then it's okay. Then, who can blame you?

Will, a.k.a. Master Lee, 40

What costumes or props work the best in bed?

Fake fur has always worked for me. Almost every woman I've been with has wanted to dress me up like a girl, so that works too.

Do's and don'ts for dirty talking?

You can call her "mommy" or "poppy," but don't use her actual mother or father's name. Do make her call you "daddy." Don't have sex when her father is in the room. Do have sex when her father is in the next room, if you do it quietly, and if you're not down South.

Under what circumstances is it okay to sleep your way to fame and fortune?

Under every circumstance except the art scene. It's like saying you're going to sleep your way to the top of the anthill.

Rachel, 24

🐱 **What tips would you give non-performers who want to woo a lover by singing or stripping or dancing?**

It's all about commitment. Any time you're second-guessing the fact that you're doing this, it's not sexy. You just have to let it go. And they should either be a total stranger or you should know them very, very well. I wouldn't advise it on the fifth date.

🐱 **What costumes or props work the best?**

I have this Mrs. Claus nightie that seemed to do the trick on several occasions.

🐱 **Do's and don'ts for dirty talking?**

You should talk about things that you know they like. If you're with a guy who really loves it when you suck his dick, you should definitely talk about sucking his dick. And go into detail. Usually if you try to get really creative with dirty talk, I've found that it doesn't work very well. It's like trying to be too creative in improv.

PERSONAL TRAINERS

Amie, 23

🐱 What are the best exercises to improve strength and endurance in the bedroom?

Studies have shown that people that exercise more have more sex; orgasms are more intense and frequent, and even last longer. Cardio helps your heart rate stay down longer, which might help you last. Strength exercises help as well. For example, if a woman has more leg strength, she may be able to ride on top longer.

🐱 What do the following fitness routines say about a person's sexual characteristics:

• A woman who only takes yoga and Pilates?
She'll be flexible in bed, energetic, and open to new things.

• A guy who goes on long runs alone?
He has stamina. He is determined, independent, and a self-starter.

• A female bodybuilder?
Most women in competitive bodybuilding use steroids to gain mass and strength. Because of this, her testosterone level may cause a variety of side effects: mood swings, back hair, enlarged clitoris, and deepened voice. But, hey, if you're into that, go for it, buddy.

🐱 Any workout gear that could double as bedroom paraphernalia?

I would avoid heavy metal objects such as barbells. But the stability ball has some great possibilities.

Sarah, 29

🦇 **What are the best exercises to do to improve strength and endurance in the bedroom?**
Yoga is excellent for the bedroom. It enhances strength, flexibility, and stamina. And the breath/body awareness can help draw you deeper into the sensations of your body and make you more aware of those of your partner. There are *bandas,* or locks, which are performed in different areas of the body. The anal lock, in which you tighten and hold the muscles of the perineum, is especially good for helping men control their erections. And deep pelvic floor exercises are super-great for women to gain extra control over their vaginal muscles.

🦇 **Tips for having anal sex for the first time?**
Anyone who wants to perform anal sex on someone else should get some lube and a correspondingly sized dildo—or a carrot if you don't have one—and try it on yourself. This will give you a good idea of what works and what doesn't.

🦇 **What are some tips for giving a good hand job?**
Remember that genetically, before we are born, male and female genitalia are the same. The head of the penis equals the clit. Treat it as such, and vice versa. Also, there is a thick long vein running up the underside of the penis which is very sensitive. Try keeping pressure on it while you move your hand up.

🦇 **Any workout gear (medicine balls, dumbbells) that could double as bedroom paraphernalia?**
Those flexible therabands one uses for stretching are great to tie people up with, and yoga blocks are great for raising different parts of the anatomy to desired positions. I suppose the smallest dumbbells could be inserted all sorts of places.

Chris, 30

What are the best exercises to improve strength and endurance in the bedroom?
Male Kegel exercises. Contract the muscles you use to take a pee. Start around 200 a day and increase to 500.

Are there any exercises I can get my boyfriend to do to improve his libido?
Squats, push-ups, lifts. Anything that challenges your body's movement will increase testosterone and, in turn, your libido. Squats especially do a lot.

What do the following fitness routines say about a person's sexual characteristics:

• A woman who only takes yoga and pilates?
Probably the more laid-back type, probably not one of the wild ones.

• A guy who goes on long runs alone?
Very long runs bring your testosterone down about 30 percent and decrease muscle mass. He's probably a thinker, maybe a Pisces type. Could be really good in bed, or a total dud, but is probably either one or the other.

• A female bodybuilder?
They have a rep for being sex freaks—very high sex drive.

• The regulars at cardio striptease class?
Very open minded—anything goes.

Jim, 32

How do you tell a significant other:

• Their body needs some serious toning?
A guy should not tell his lady that her body needs some "toning." Being this blunt is asking for trouble. The best thing to do is include her in your workouts. If it's a woman telling a man, she can just say, "Get in shape, or I will not have sex with your untoned ass."

• Their oral sex technique needs improving?
Guys have to understand that the super-speed-tongue-across-the-pussy, as seen in porn, does not work in the real world. Slow and steady works best. Lick around the pussy, kiss and lick the inner thighs, lick the crease of the leg. Be prepared to stay down there awhile. Good oral sex should take about twenty to twenty-five minutes.

• Any sexy exercise videos to get me in shape and in the mood?
For the ladies, the Tae-Bo stuff with Billy Blanks. Guys, just watch women's volleyball on ESPN.

What are some tips for giving a good hand job?
Stand directly behind your man—in front of a mirror is very hot—or lie right beside him in the bed. Grab his cock. Start pumping it up and down, slowly at first, then a little faster. If he places his hand over yours and follows your motion, let him assist. You can be a little rough with it; hell knows we are.

Noyah, 32

🐱 **What are the best exercises to do to improve strength and endurance in the bedroom?**

The sex itself will take care of the strength and endurance; it's the aftereffects you need to worry about, like a tight back and a sore neck. So while your partner is making coffee, make sure you do a cross stretch (left knee bends to the right and vice versa), a hamstring stretch, and hug your knees to your chest.

🐱 **What's a good way to turn someone down after you've had sex with them once, and once was enough?**

Reverse psychology. Call them back, tell them you're available anytime. Offer to let them move in. You'll never hear from them again.

🐱 **Are there any exercises my boyfriend can do to improve his libido?**

I have two words for you: bench presses. It works like magic. The act of pushing weight up and down just gets guys going.

🐱 **Is it ever okay to hook up with a client?**

As a general rule, it's best not to hook up with people who pay your rent. Resisting come-ons is tricky, but playing dumb and talking about ligament inflammation usually does the trick.

🐱 **Any workout gear that could double as bedroom paraphernalia?**

I've always thought that inner-thigh chair could be put to better use.

Sex Advice From

PET STORE CLERKS

Shawn, 31

🍂 What sexual tendencies/characteristic do you associate with the following pet owners?

• A man and a bichon frise?
I think the man with the big dog might be compensating for his small penis, so the man with the small dog might be compensating for his big penis.

• A woman and a Great Dane?
Um, I guess she wants a dog with a big dick.

• A man and a greyhound?
He's probably compassionate.

• Anyone with a pug?
I know a lot of people with pugs, and I don't want to say anything mean about them.

🍂 You've been dating someone for six months. You have sex once a week. Is that too little?

That's way too little. Unless it's really good sex to keep you through the rest of the week. At least four times a week would be good—and not all in one night.

🍂 Have you experienced female ejaculation, and if so, what brought it about?

No. But I heard about this girl who did. I was trying to hook up with her, so I could feel her spew all over my belly, but I just couldn't hook anything up. I wish I had a story like that.

Jesse, 24

🐱 **Is your job a good way to meet sex partners?**

No. Well, I'm seeing someone right now. But even if I weren't, a lot of people who come into pet stores are really pet obsessed, and that's because they don't have anyone else in their lives. I have two cats, but I am by no means pet obsessed.

🐱 **My dog is one jealous bitch. Whenever I bring a date home, she tries to kill them. What should I do?**

Is this also a studio apartment? I would try to introduce the two of them. Some dogs are especially sensitive to the sounds of sex, like it sounds like someone's getting hurt. Definitely try to introduce the date to the dog and let them bond before you start doing it.

🐱 **If you had to use one item from your store during sex, what would it be and how would you use it?**

Sex with riding boots would be fun. I'm not so much into whipping or anything. I would maybe use some chain collars to tie up whoever I was with. It would have to be someone that I felt very intimate and safe with.

What's the best anal technique?

I've had guys tell me that the easiest way is if the girl is on top sitting backwards, if she has a lot of lube and controls the pace of it. I'm not really into it, because I had it when I was young with this guy who was a real asshole. But I do think anal stimulation during oral sex is good.

Male bisexuality: myth or reality?

A reality. I went out with this guy a while ago that would occasionally jack off his friend but was also into women. I don't know how that's not bisexual.

POOL CLEANERS

Shaun, 22

Is it true what adult videos suggest about pool cleaners—that you have the coolest job in the whole world?

Definitely one of the best. I'd say one, firefighter; two, UPS guy; three, pool man.

My girlfriend found my porn collection and is upset. What should I tell her?

"Someday, these will be collector's items."

What's the best pickup line you've used or heard?

I just went to a U2 concert and wore a shirt that said "Mind if I touch your butt?" It worked six times. I also had a friend who would go into a bar and say to someone, "From now until we leave, I'm going to tell you nothing but lies." Jesus Christ, the guy got laid more than I do.

Bill, 51

Is it true what adult videos suggest about pool cleaners—that you have the coolest job in the whole world?
It doesn't suck. I'd rate it number five for automatically getting laid by what you do for a living. There are better jobs, but it happens. You're out there, you're hot and sweaty, you're in your underwear. You'd have to be a complete retard not to get laid every once in a while. It's mostly women at home, while their men are out working.

My girlfriend is interested in a threesome with another guy, and I'm open to it, but I'm afraid of being outperformed. What's your advice?
Don't pick a pool guy. Get a nice accountant or an artist or the guy who works at Starbucks. A pool guy will burn you down.

What's the best pickup line you've used or heard?
"You look like my first wife."

Sex in the water seems like fun, but it seems to require lubricant after a while. Any tips?
I don't like having sex in the pool. It's lousy. It starts to squeak after a while. You can hear it.

Bob, 55

**Is it true what adult videos suggest about pool cleaners—
that you have the coolest job in the whole world?**
We'd have the coolest job in the world if the movies were the way it really happens.
It's never happened. Maybe I've just been too much of a businessman to let it.

What's the best pickup line you've used or heard?
Just say, "Hi, how are you?" Don't pull out all those movie lines.

**My girlfriend found my porn collection and is upset. What
should I tell her?**
You can always say, "Let's sit down and watch one together."

Sex Advice From

PROJECTIONISTS

Kenji, 24

You're taking a girl to the movies, and you're hoping for a sexy night. Should you see an action film, romance, comedy, or drama?
Romance.

What is the least sexy movie of all time?
Starship Troopers.

What movie is an instant aphrodisiac?
Original Sin, with Antonio Banderas and Angelina Jolie. A lot of girls really like Angelina Jolie.

Projecting a film is a very specific and delicate process. What can your job teach the rest of us about sex?
Finger dexterity.

Chuck, 34
....

🎞 Ever had sex in the projection booth?

Oh, yeah. If you've been in the business for more than two or three years and you're sexually active, it had to have happened at some point. I think 99 percent of projectionists have done something.

🎞 You're taking a girl to the movies, and you're hoping for a sexy night. What kind of movie should you see?

A romantic film is risky: the leading actor might be more attractive than you. A comedy could work. I mean, *American Pie,* no. But any Tom Hanks comedy would probably work.

🎞 What is the least sexy movie of all time?

Showgirls is pretty high on the list. I'd say anything with Schwarzenegger in it. Actually, the worst is *The Specialist,* with Sylvester Stallone and Sharon Stone, two people so horribly past their prime, trying to get it on in the shower.

🎞 What's your favorite sexy movie?

A Fish Called Wanda is actually kind of a hot little film. Watching Jamie Lee Curtis writhe around on the floor is always a good thing.

🎞 What can your job teach the rest of us about sex?

Well, attention to detail. And preparation is a big thing too. Keep your equipment clean. The funny thing about projection is that the better job I do, the less the audience notices I'm around. So in a way, it's like inversely proportional to sex: the better you are, the more your partner's going to remember that you're there.

Noel, 27

🐱 **You're taking a guy to the movies, and you're hoping for a sexy night. What should you see?**
With 90 percent of men, comedy or action is the best choice. Laughter or testosterone will put him in the mood.

🐱 **What is the least sexy movie of all time?**
Waterworld.

🐱 **What cinematic scenes have you played out in bed? Are there some you'd like to try?**
I've never reenacted any. I thought the scenes between Mark Ruffalo and Meg Ryan in *In the Cut* were pretty hot. Also, the scene in *The Bridges of Madison County* where Meryl's gossipy neighbor phones her right as she's about to sit down with Clint and she can't get rid of her. As she's standing behind him, she adjusts his collar. Oh baby!

🐱 **Projecting a film is a very specific and delicate process. What can your job teach the rest of us about sex?**
Lubrication is essential. And proper roller alignment.

John, 22

You're taking a girl to the movies, and you're hoping for a sexy night. Should you see an action film, a romance, a comedy, or a drama?

I'd say a romantic comedy. Something involving Tom Hanks or Meg Ryan.

You wouldn't be bored?

I think you sacrifice an hour here for an hour later, do you know what I'm saying?

Ever had sex in the projection booth?

I once received and gave oral sex in the projection booth. It was on the splicing table, if that helps you.

I like to fantasize about other guys when I have sex. I think my partner fantasizes about other girls. Is the relationship doomed?

No, I think there should just be open communication. An easy way to start this is to talk about reenacting a movie scene, where maybe there are two or three partners of the same sex in the scene, and try to incorporate that into your relationship.

Any particular scenes in mind?

I think the easiest way to do this, especially if you want your partner to bring along another girl, is ask to reenact the scene from *Wild Things*—the one with Neve Campbell and Denise Richards and that lucky, lucky bastard. I don't even remember who it was.

 What cinematic scenes have you played out in bed? Are there any you'd like to try?

I've always kind of wanted to finish off the scene in the third *Austin Powers* film where he's with the two twins in Catholic schoolgirl uniforms, but I haven't gotten there yet. Someday, someday.

What can your job teach the rest of us about sex?

The projection booth gets very steamy; the air conditioning never really cools down the heat lamps that work in there. Especially when a film burns or breaks, and you are in the projection booth—which can be upwards of 110, 115 degrees—it's important to stick with it, because there's really nothing else you can do but finish what you started. And I think that's important with sex. No matter how hard it gets and how hot it gets, you've always gotta finish what you start.

PUBLICISTS

Aimee, 30

🦇 How can I recover from the sexual PR disaster of having my sex tape discovered by my roommate?

Pull a Paris Hilton and profit from your taped sexcapades by adding a viewing fee to your roomie's share of the cable bill.

🦇 What about giving someone an STD?

Since it's something the receiver would want to keep quiet, too, there's not much risk of word spreading around town (and, now that you know, you shouldn't be spreading anything else around, either). Unless of course, you are a rock star and someone creates a blog called yournameheregavemeherpes.com. Then you're fucked. And probably not fucking too many groupies after that.

🦇 What can I do to drum up good publicity to impress my latest crush?

A good word-of-mouth campaign works well. Depending on the crush, a word-of-mouth-skills campaign may work even better.

🦇 What's the number one thing everyone should have in their sex drawer (other than condoms and lube)?

Handcuffs. Make that two things—handcuffs and the keys.

Bruce, 31

🔥 **How can I recover from the sexual PR disaster of publicly and drunkenly hooking up at a bar in front of my colleagues?**
I absolutely recommend joking about the slip of tongue the following morning—first thing, so you beat others to the punch.

🔥 **What about cheating on a well-liked boyfriend or girlfriend?**
Don't deny or confirm. Just move forward.

🔥 **What's the number one thing everyone should have in their sex drawer (other than condoms and lube)?**
Porn, Mary J, erotic poetry, naked self-portraits, and a copy of *Moby Dick*.

🔥 **What dress-up game is the most fun to play in the bedroom?**
An officer and a gentleman.

Sarah, 30

🐚 **What can I do to drum up good publicity to impress my hot new neighbor?**
Definitely try to look cute at all hours, going to the gym and the grocery store, doing your laundry. And be friendly to everyone in the building. A guy in my building just said to me, "You're like the mayor of this building."

🐚 **I keep running into this guy I had a drunken one-night stand with two years ago. I still get really weird around him. Should I mention the one-night stand or pretend it didn't happen?**
Pretend that it didn't happen—total nonchalance. You're fabulous, you're wonderful; why are you freaking out? That's how I would act every single time.

🐚 **I'm pretty lazy and selfish in the sack. Is there any way I can be a great lay with minimal effort?**
I think if you're a woman, the missionary position can work for that. Missionary, then just make a lot of noise—because then you're making them go crazy. A guy always has to work, but a guy always wants to work.

QUEER ROCKERS

Chris, 22

What instrument turns you on the most and why?
Cello. Cuz it sits in between the legs and rides up like a giant penis. I haven't had the opportunity to use one during sex. I've masturbated to pictures of this hot motherfucker playing his cello. He was first seat. And German. And hot.

What advice do you have for groupies who want to fuck you?
Just be somewhat hot and really aggressive. I'm pretty easy.

I'm a gay man desperately in love with straight guys. How do you recommend seducing them?
People make the mistake of thinking that the seducee needs to be terribly intoxicated in order to be seduced. While that certainly helps, I've found it's easier the more intoxicated the seducer is. Cuz then you've got more balls about seducing. Get trashed and just go for it. This will work at least 80 percent of the time. Trust me.

I'm tired of the same sexual positions everyone knows. Tell me something that isn't in books with titles like Sexual Positions 101.
This one isn't too original but it is my favorite. I like sitting on the dick while I get fucked. And then leaning back with my hands on the bed behind me. Even though I'm usually a bottom, I mostly like to be on top while being a bottom. It feels best.

My boyfriend says I suck at giving head.
Start out easy. Get some spit stored up in your mouth and drool it onto his dick while you suck on it. The wetter the better. Then also make sure you lick his balls in between blowing him. Also, swallow his come. It's hot to swallow.

Lynne, 26   Simone, 29

What instrument turns you on the most and why?
Simone: I'd say bass is the sexiest. It must have something to do with the heavy vibrations.

Do you ever use beer bottles to stimulate yourself and if so what brand?
Lynne: No. That sounds dangerous to me. Haven't you ever heard that urban legend where the girl has to get 176 stitches and pee out a straw forever and ever?

And haven't you read the new Mötley Crüe confessional where they force some poor, poor groupie to sit on a beer bottle for the whole set and then—only then—can she have sex with the whole band? And then the poor thing has to have sex with Mötley fucking Crüe! That's fucking rough. But personally, I'd choose Budweiser. I'm drinkin' one right now in fact. Although it is in a can, and that seems more dangerous somehow. But I in no way endorse sticking anything glass and bottle shaped inside any orifice of anyone, unless there is a good reason and everyone is willing. Please be safe, people.

I'm a straight guy who loves anal stimulation. My girlfriend thinks that enjoying anal stimulation is automatically gay. What can I say to her to assure her I love her and women but enjoy getting it up the ass every once in a while?
Simone: That's hot, dude. If she doesn't get it, there are plenty of hot ladies, queer and straight, willing to take you from behind. Let's not forget, dildos have no gender.

Lynne: Say, "I love you and women but I enjoy getting it up the ass every once in a while." If she refuses, *dump her.* Sorry, but she is misinformed, stuck in the dark age, and obviously sexually b-to-the-o-r-i-n-g. Move on.

🐱 **Are there any songs or albums that you think can induce orgasms?**
Lynne: "Burnin' Up," Madonna.

🐱 **I used to be a lesbian; now I'm happily married to a man with one child. All my friends tease me and call me a four-year queer (I was only gay during college). What can I tell them to shut them the fuck up?**
Simone: According to my roomie May, straight is the new gay. We're in a post-gay, sexuality-is-a-lot-more-fluid-than-you-think period of history. If they can't hang, you need to get yourself a new homo gang with broader horizons, girl.

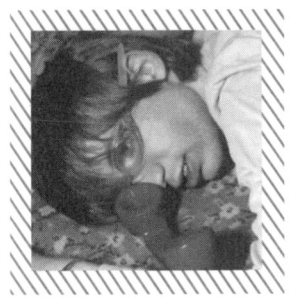

Christopher, a.k.a. "Absentee," 22

What advice do you have for groupies who want to fuck you?
Firstly, don't have tits. They sure are pretty sometimes, but they do nothing for me. Make obscure references to foreign films, as this has worked in the past. (Almodovar is my current favorite, but someone caught me in my Bergman phase and was successful.) Also, I'm a shy one when not being a frenzied mess on stage, so try making the first move after buying me a drink.

I'm a straight guy who loves anal stimulation. My girlfriend thinks that enjoying anal stimulation is automatically gay. What can I say to her to assure her I love her and women but enjoy getting it up the ass every once in a while?
Buy a strap-on and explain that mutual penetration is the safest bet for maintaining a balanced and healthy relationship. Tell her that you heard this on Dr. Phil. Women trust Dr. Phil.

Are there any songs or albums that you think can induce orgasms?
I once dated this guy who had a slightly unhealthy obsession with Wolf Eyes. There's something about utter aural violence that motivates one to fuck like there's no tomorrow.

I have a problem: I constantly have an erection. What music can you recommend that will finally put my boner to sleep?

Limp Bizkit. (Nothing turns me on less than guys who act like they have huge cocks. They don't.)

What is a buzz kill that happens way too frequently that people should be aware of?

Please turn your cell phones to the off position.

What advice can you offer me on how to get chicks? I'm in my twenties, reasonably attractive, and I never get laid.

1. Wear clothes that fit. (Ever heard of a little phenomenon called metrosexuality?)

2. Act disinterested.

3. Learn to dance while looking disinterested.

Sex Advice From

RECORD STORE CLERKS

Ryan, 25

What albums would you recommend for sex?
DJ Shadow's *Endtroducing* is a good record. Marvin Gaye's *Let's Get It On*.

What's the best way to persuade your partner to try anal sex?
Just ask her if she's ever tried it. It's worked for me before. It doesn't hurt to ask. That's the part that definitely won't hurt.

What's a no-fail cunnilingus technique?
Watch pornos, man. They know how to do it. I guess the thing to remember is that every girl is different.

What drug is the best supplement to sex?
Weed, probably. I dunno. Ecstasy is retarded. You're like, "Water is awesome," "I love smelling." It's stupid.

If a girl reveals herself as a massive fan of Sting's solo work, should you still sleep with her?
Fuck, no! Sting is the Antichrist. Same goes for Phil Collins. She could get away with, like, the first Police record, maybe. I'd have more respect for her if she were really into Bell Biv Devoe. Actually, that's my third record! *Poison* by Bell Biv Devoe. Now that's a sexual album. The last few tracks on that record? Raunchy. Same with R. Kelly. He rocks innuendo like no other. A lot of respect for him, man.

How long should sex last?
Y'know, the optimum is between five and ten minutes. I'm going to say seven minutes.

Mikey, 27

What albums would you recommend for a night of sex?

Portishead's *Dummy*. *Black Celebration* by Depeche Mode. Anything by Barry White, of course. Something about it just feels so right.

What's the most diplomatic way to show your partner how to improve their oral sex technique?

Keep it in the moment. Don't manually show them what to do; in my experience, that's a bad way to go. In a roundabout way, kind of say, "Oh, you know what would really feel good?" Never say, "You are doing that all wrong," "Stop it," or "I want to go to sleep." Emphasize only the positives.

What's the key to truly great sex?

Spontaneity. Sexual relationships are sort of rote behavior, you know? You come over, eat, watch a movie, go to bed, and then you have sex. When you least expect it to happen . . . there should be lots of that.

What is the optimal duration for sexual intercourse?

I'd say an hour. As I've matured as a lover, I've found that it's better to savor the act as a whole instead of fixating upon the release.

What's your no-fail cunnilingus technique?

Writing the letters of the alphabet with the tip of the tongue.

What if the girl is dyslexic?

Good one. Okay, well, I guess I'd say keep it varied. Variety!

Sex Advice From

ROLLER DERBY GIRLS

Tami, a.k.a. Sybil Disobedience, 32

🐱 What's the biggest mistake a guy can make in bed?

If you're doing something, and she likes that thing, don't stop doing that thing for anything in the world. I hate when you're really close, and then suddenly they start doing something different, and you're like, "Nooooo! Why?! Why?! Why?! Why?! You ruined it! It's over!"

🐱 So what are some tips for keeping a long-distance relationship hot?

Phone sex. Internet. Webcams. All that stuff. I think people are getting a lot more open about those sorts of things. I am always surprised at the number of people I know who commonly show their private parts on Webcams.

🐱 What piece of roller-derby equipment would you bring into the bedroom?

This question has come up a bunch of times: "Have you had sex with your pads on yet?" I think the obvious application goes with kneepads and blow jobs. Some people seem to be really turned on by the notion of body armor. I think if you're naked with the exception of these pads, it's a little weird.

🐱 What's a good vibrator?

It's called the Ultime. It's blue, and it's curved, basically like a boomerang. It's got a big knobby head that totally hits you in the G-spot. Revolutionized my life. Other than that, the rabbit. I broke my rabbit in half, literally.

Joey Hardcore, 22

🦪 When planning a threesome, is it better to ask quasi-friends or to scout out attractive strangers?

I'm of the opinion that threesomes that you construct are just not a good idea. There are couples that have chemistry and should be having sex; there are groups of three people who have chemistry and should all be having sex together. And when you try and force it, it's just kind of lame.

🦪 Any tips for pubic hair removal or maintenance?

I'd say go with the Mach 3 razor. The Mach 3: hot. I generally take a hot bath first and then soak and then use that. But my skin isn't really sensitive. I know a lot of people who get ingrown hairs all the time, no matter what they do.

🦪 Do you have a preference about your partners' pubic hair?

Yes and no. I mean, I'm not going to turn anyone away. I prefer girls shaven and guys unshaven. With girls, hair kind of gets in the way. Shaven guys just look weird.

Male bisexuality: myth or reality?

It's a reality. I used to be really into bi guys, and a boy I dated for a really long time was definitely bisexual.

How can someone give the best blow job?

By asking. I'm not into the idea that there's a universal way to do anything right. Even something as simple as hand jobs—I can think of three different boys who told me three radically different ways to do it, from squeezing the head to squeezing the shaft to lightly rubbing like my fingers in a circle over the head.

Sarah, a.k.a. Lady Batterly, 24

🦇 What's the best method for fingering someone?
Have a general clue about the clitoris. A common mistake, especially when you're younger, is to stroke it too hard. Also, lubrication is important.

🦇 When you're going down on a girl, what should you do besides clit stimulation?
God, it seems like so many guys are just bad at it in general, and I don't know why. They think that fingering you is going to make it fine. You have to be fluid and keep a rhythm. Don't just jam things in there. And don't lick all over like a crazy person.

🦇 Tips for keeping a long-distance relationship hot?
Make out with people at a bar and don't tell them about it.

🦇 What roller-derby equipment would you bring into the bedroom?
Kneepads, elbow pads, and skates would make a really good combination.

Cecilia, a.k.a. CC Bullets, 31

🐱 **Is it okay to think about other people or situations other than what I'm doing right now when I'm with my partner?**
Fantasizing is a natural thing—we're all humans. Sometimes a little fantasy, as long as you don't act on it, is okay. Life is too short; why do you have to be careful with what you're thinking?

🐱 **Tips for pubic hair removal and maintenance?**
Wax, baby, wax! I also shave. If you don't have a long-term relationship, and you're just going on a date or you're just doing it once in a while with a new person, I'd say shaving is okay, because then you can let it grow out. Otherwise I'd say wax, because shaving gives you those little bumpies.

🐱 **What are some things that you can do while going down on a girl to make oral sex more enjoyable?**
Grabbing the tits is great.

🐱 **What are some tips you'd say for giving someone the best blow job?**
Keep a rhythmic motion, make some noise, and use a lot of suction.

Sex Advice From

ROMANCE
NOVELISTS

Lisa Kleypas, age withheld

🦇 **What's the best position to employ when having sex in a closet?**

This is a dilemma frequently faced by lords and ladies of Regency historical romances, and also by modern-day parents of small children. Speaking as one of the latter category, I can say with authority that the configuration of your closet will most likely determine your position, and I must caution you to the perils of stray hangers and shoes.

Alisa Kwitney, 40

If a man asks a woman how many men she's slept with, should she answer?

She should say seven, if she's twenty-five or under. Seven's a nice number. It allows for a few boyfriends, a couple of holiday flings, and assorted lapses in judgment. The principle here is the same one you use when declaring what you bought in France on vacation to the IRS: you want to be honest, but within reason. If the woman's thirty-five or under, she can safely acknowledge fifteen.

What sex toys do you recommend?

Every woman should have more than one tube of lipstick, more than one pair of nice heels, and more than one vibrator. I'm not sure what men should have, but as I recall from *Portnoy's Complaint,* they can manage quite well with a piece of liver.

When tensions are high in a relationship, how do you set the mood for a romantic night at home?

Up the ante with a fabricated crisis that affects both of you. For example, scream that the castle is under attack, shove a chair against the door, and demand some just-in-case-I-die sex. Of course, there's always couples therapy if the siege doesn't work.

🦇 Is it okay to fantasize about other people when you're in bed with your partner?

It's absolutely fine to fantasize that your lover is a Navy SEAL, a dangerous pirate, Lord Aragorn, or even Colin Powell, if that's the way your bread gets buttered. If, however, you keep fantasizing that you're in bed with Morty Greenberg who sits across from you at work, then you might have a problem on your hands.

🦇 What's a good way for a first-timer to ease into dirty talk?

I suggest that a first-timer cover the same progression that romance writers have followed from the eighties to the present, moving from terms such as "manhood" and "the flower of her femininity" to "throbbing shaft" and "sensitive bud." The term "erection" has a certain giddy charm. But be advised: no term has yet been coined for the female genitalia that does not sound overly medical, overly pornographic, or overly precious. (Unless you can say "pussy" like Antonio Banderas does in *Shrek 2*.)

Sex Advice From

SANTAS

Brittonie, 23

🎅 **I hooked up with a colleague at work. Now it seems to have fizzled out quite naturally, and another guy at that job is interested in me. Is it a bad idea to double-dip?**
No. As long as you can keep the nookie out of the workplace and the workplace out of the sex, there should be no problem.

🎅 **When is it okay to hook up with a friend's ex?**
Depends on how good a friend it is. If it's a really good friend, I would say you should ask them. I made the mistake of hooking up with a friend's ex-boyfriend and it ruined our friendship. It just wasn't worth it. It's kind of like hooking up with your best friend. You have to weigh the consequences.

🎅 **Is it appropriate to give someone a sex toy for Christmas? What is the best sex toy to give for Christmas?**
I gave one of my friends a blow-up doll—it was more of a joke than anything else. Several years ago my friend and I exchanged gifts. I got her a clit kisser, and she got me jelly.

🎅 **I'm a girl whose boyfriend is bisexual. I'm not interested in threesomes, and I prefer to be monogamous. Is there hope for our relationship?**
Sure. You can either say, "Don't make out with boys while we're together." Or, "I want to watch."

Jamie, 30

My fuck buddy and I have very little to talk about, and while this wasn't a problem at first, now it's kind of turning me off when we're physical. How can I get him to be more of a buddy and thus a better fuck?

Share a sex partner with that other person. Then you could reflect on what that experience was like for you both.

A guy I'm seeing can only finish with a condom on if he takes me from behind. I'm starting to take the lack of face time personally. He does a lot to please me, so is this something I should just get over?

I actually had a Santa that was like this. We lined the room with mirrors. You get the face-to-face time that you're looking for, and it gives you the sensation of having two or three other Santas in the room, without actually having to get into multiplayer action.

I've gone out with a guy twice. We flirt and touch a lot and have a lot of fun, but he still hasn't made a pass at me. Is he not interested? What should I do to make him more interested?

That's a difficult question; a lot of people have different tastes. If it's a man and you're trying to get his attention, the smartest thing to do is to grab him by the hand, whisper some dirty comments into his ear, pull him into the bathroom, and give him a blow job. You'll find out in only a couple of minutes where you stand.

Yomi, 40

I'm spending Christmas with my girlfriend—at her family's house. Any advice for sneaking in some sex without accidental walk-ins?
Sneak off to the bathroom—say you have a problem with your contact lens and need someone to give you a hand. One of my favorites is "I've got something in the car."

How do I avoid awkwardness and clichés when I want to invite someone up to my apartment after a date?
The best line I was given was, "Well, let's see if you're a good fuck."

I really want to have a threesome, but all of the people I've met that want to have threesomes are disgusting. How can I go about finding a couple of normal people for this?
The best thing: go to a gay bar and pick up a man. There are lots of men in gay bars who aren't necessarily gay and are open-minded enough to try something like that.

Sex Advice From

SEX SHOP EMPLOYEES

Molly, 25

🦋 What beginner sex toys do you recommend ?

Well, I must begin with the important disclaimer that every person is unique and likes something different. I recommend picking an internal/external vibe like the Gigolo or Lava Lust. They tend to last a long time, and smooth vibrations can be enjoyed on the clit, around the vulva and inside, too! If I were a dude, I'd buy the vulva Fleshlight. It's a cyberskin masturbation sleeve that looks and feels fabulous.

🦋 Can you recommend some porn for a beginning viewer?

Into hetero movies? Try *Urban Friction*. The movie has an actual plot, following a couple of punk, tattooed cuties trying to incorporate threesomes into their sex life. Not into hetero movies? Check out *Pornograflics* for an array of genders and sexy vignettes.

🦋 What digital stimulation works best on women?

Fingers are probably the best sex toy. We've seen fingers going crazy in porn, but that rigorous single finger going back and forth directly on the clit is not the answer for most. Try different things and ask for explicit feedback. Try rubbing vertically outside the labia slowly or circular movements around the clit and above the clitoral hood. Try three flat fingers up and down the entire vulva and gently slide one lubricated finger in between the inner lips and right over the vaginal opening. Shoving in more than one finger immediately is not okay. Start slow, one finger at a time, and add as she opens up.

Kim, 46

What beginner sex toy do you recommend for women?
The Judy Jetson. It's a nice sparkly purple jelly rubber with great vibrations. Wonderful for internal as well as external use. The tapered end is great for women starting out.

For men?
A cock ring, especially the vibrating Honeyspot, which pleases both partners. It's touch-activated and will vibrate the woman's clit during the in-and-out, especially if she's riding cowgirl on top.

Can you recommend some porn for a beginning viewer?
You want a plot line, Veronica Hart's videos are great. She's a talented director and scriptwriter, which is reflected in her work. There's lots of sex and it usually doesn't disintegrate into the "bobbing, hairy man butt" thing.

Female ejaculation: how can you make it happen?
Crooking the fingers in a "come here" motion while plunging in and out of the vagina, not too hard, will stimulate the G-spot area immensely. When masturbating, I like to use the middle and ring fingers of my right hand.

Tips on giving a good blow job?
Using your tongue a lot. It will take the tension out of your jaw and give his dick a whole new sensation. Vary the way you use your tongue on him, from fat, sloppy licks to sharply pointed tongue tip circles. And don't forget the balls.

Becca, 23

What beginner sex toy do you recommend for women?

For women, I think a great starter toy is a variable speed or multifunction vibrator—internal or external—and plenty of lube.

For men?

For men, I'd recommend a basic male masturbation sleeve, like the Hand Job Stroker or Crystal Gal, and plenty of lube as well. I also recommend a beginner (smaller) anal toy, since prostate stimulation can be really intense for a lot of men. This can be a touchy subject. I like to point out that body parts don't have a sexuality. As in, if you're straight, how can your ass be gay?

Say I wanted to introduce swinging or involving additional sex partners. How should I approach the subject with my partner?

First think about whether your relationship is strong enough and honest enough to survive it. If you are thinking of it as something that can revive a struggling relationship, you need to think again. If you're sure you're ready, be sure to frame it in a positive way. Don't say, "Honey, I'm really bored with our sex life. Maybe we should try swinging so I can screw other people who are better in the sack than you."

Sex Advice From

SEXUALITY
PROFESSORS

Sandra Caron, 47

🦇 **What's the biggest sexual taboo in America, and should it be broken?**
It's still not okay to talk about sex. We need to educate people about the importance of that. We really do need to be much more open to the fact that our sexuality is part of who we are.

🦇 **My girlfriend thinks there's something wrong with her because she hasn't been able to orgasm through penetration. What can I do to help her have an orgasm through vaginal sex?**
The myth that there is only one right way to have an orgasm is ridiculous. She needs to investigate her body so she understands how it works. Then she can show her partner what feels good, so the partner can be part of that.

🦇 **What's the most common mistake men/women make during sex?**
Not paying enough attention to the other person's desires and really clueing in to what feels good. They may just go for things without even checking out "Does this feel good for this person? Is this something they will enjoy?"

🦇 **When sleeping with your significant other, is it okay to think about other people or scenarios to facilitate an orgasm?**
Lots of people do that. Right or wrong, it just is. I'd try to accept that, for you, this is what works, and you're with this person for a reason because you care about them or whatever. Try to move on from there.

Dennis M. Dailey, 66

What non-Western attitude about sex should be adopted in this country?

The Hindu perspective, which recognizes pleasure is okay, not wrong, stupid, bad, sick, dumb, or ugly.

What's the most common mistake men and women make during sex?

"Spectatoring," where we're so worried about who we are, what we are, how we look, and how good we are, that we, in essence, jump outside of our body, stand over in the corner and watch ourselves having sex, making all kinds of judgments and comments while we're doing it.

The best way to tell someone they give bad head without hurting their feelings?

You can't tell somebody that without hurting their feelings! What you can do is say to a person, "Look, I've had some experiences with getting blow jobs. I know that I like things a certain way. There's no reason that I should expect you to know what I want and what I need, so let me teach you, let me guide you."

Is it okay to think about other people/scenarios when hooking up with your significant other in an effort to facilitate an orgasm?

Sure. It wouldn't be any different than watching videotapes, fantasizing about the sunset, or whatever rings your chime. Fantasies are not real. That's why fantasies are so nice. We can do all that stuff and not get arrested.

SIDESHOW PERFORMERS

Scott, age withheld

What sexual feat can I perform to impress a new lover?
I've always believed that oral prowess is an incredible specialty. Also, when a
woman goes for a guy's armpits or nipples, things really get exciting. It's when
a woman knows that a man's body is responsive in areas other than just genitalia.

**What sexual characteristics would you attribute to some-
one who is covered in piercings?**
Oh, probably very daring, especially if they have a pierced clit. It says that they
appreciate the sensuality that can be created through modification and apprecia-
tion of their own body.

Someone who eats competitively?
I would think he would probably have some problems internally. And he's probably more into the contest of eating than he is into pleasing a lover.

Someone who swallows swords?
Well, being one who does, it doesn't necessarily mean that you know what to do
with a penis or a vagina; it means you know what to do with a sword. Although
gag reflex diminishment can be terrific, I know people who wouldn't dream of
swallowing a sword who give the best head.

**I'm interested in trying S&M with someone I am casually
dating. What's the best way to break the ice?**
Go through a delicate fetish phase, getting into foot worship or body worship—
because S&M can cover a lot of areas. I was dating a porn star who wanted me to
make her butt red. She said, "Really spank my ass." And she would become
orgasmic when I would do it, really become a waterworks, and I said, "This, I like."

Diamond Donny V., 26

What sexual feat can I perform to impress a new lover?
The Rear Admiral: take your sweetheart by the rear, bend at the waist, and using your member, steer her around, preferably into furniture or down a flight of stairs.

What can someone in an audience do to let you know while you're onstage that they'd like to meet later?
Clap, and laugh at all the stupid jokes. Write "love you" on your eye lids and bat them. Make lewd gestures denoting oral sex, or just pop that glass eye out and throw it at me.

What's a sexual practice everyone should try once before they die?
Autoerotic asphyxiation. Who knows? It may be the sexual practice you try *right* before you die.

Heather, 19

🐱 **What sexual characteristics would you attribute to someone who is covered in piercings?**
Looks are probably deceiving; they're probably going to be very plain.

🐱 **Someone who eats competitively?**
They're probably very nibbly, going for the toes, really weird stuff. It would probably freak me out.

🐱 **Someone who can bend in unusual ways?**
Huh, well, that—that's pretty self-explanatory.

🐱 **Someone who swallows swords?**
Well—ahem—yeah, you know—the greatest ability to deep throat ever.

🐱 **I'm interested in trying S&M with someone I am casually dating. What's the best way to break the ice?**
I'd probably start it off as a teasing joke, testing the waters, seeing how it flows with them.

Sex Advice From

SKATEBOARDERS

Shannon, age withheld

🐱 Describe your ideal personal X Games.

I like a man to be physical. I dated an underwear model once and one time he stood up with my legs wrapped around him and he fucked me that way. It was hot! The funnest thing I've done was with two guys at once, so I could suck one guy while I was done from behind, doggy style.

🐱 And how many times have you done that?

Twice. I've had sex with two girls before but that's not as much fun.

🐱 Could you find a guy attractive because he hasn't had much experience?

Yeah. I de-virginized a guy because he told me he was a virgin. I wasn't even attracted to him, but I thought, "This guy's a virgin!"

🐱 What are some specific ways to keep a long-term sexual relationship fresh?

Remain mysterious. Do not divulge too much information. For me, mystery is key.

🐱 Is there a way to incorporate porn into sex in a way that doesn't seem cheesy and can be exciting for both partners?

Porn's hot. That's something I did recently with this guy I'm dating. We watch porn together and have really great sex. Hollywood movies like *9½ Weeks* just don't turn me on. Specific titles: *The Voyeur 22* by John Leslie and *Cherry Hawk*.

🐱 Are there any words that should never be used to refer to genitalia?

"Roast beef curtains."

Roberto, age withheld

Name a specific move that enhances oral sex?
I call it the three-point plan. While using the mouth, you have to use two other parts of the body at the same time.

What are your personal X Games: a sex trick with an especially high degree of difficulty?
Well, I can do the Hercules-One-Arm-Bed-to-Bed-Transfer. That's where you're having sex and you grab her underneath with one arm and you pick her up from there without breaking the flow and take her to another room, and maybe hit the wall first. You just have to do it with one arm. And if you do it right they say, "Oh, my god!" You show them the strength you got and they like it.

What are the most common sex-related injuries?
Blue balls, and a stiff neck and tongue.

Do you have a good remedy?
For blue balls, you either spank it, or put on a Jacques Cousteau hat. One time, I had blue balls and my friend took a sock and rolled it up, kind of like a donut, and said, "Put this on." And I put this little Jacques Cousteau hat on, and that helped it.

What's one rule of sexual etiquette that should never be broken?

Never talk about what you did with a girl in front of her. They just don't want to feel like a slut, even if they are one.

What are some specific ways to keep a long-term sexual relationship fresh?

Batteries. Take her different places, not always in the bed. Don't show her everything you've got in the beginning. Always reserve one little trick.

Are there any words that should never be used to refer to genitalia?

"Dangling participle," for a guy. And obviously not "cunt." You better be a black belt if you're gonna use that one. Never call it "carne asada." You won't be getting none of that shit.

Quynn, 33

What skate move is guaranteed to get me laid?
Oh, *No Comply*. It's an old-school move that involves, well, spreading your legs.

What's the best way to pick someone up at a skate park?
Say, "Wow, you make it look so easy." And just kind of stand there in awe.

How can you ask someone to be your fuck buddy?
Say, "This isn't really working out, but can I still come over on Tuesdays and Fridays?" I think that would be awesome. I actually was just thinking of saying that like two weeks ago, because I was seeing someone and it wasn't working out.

How can I spice up a run-of-the-mill hand job?
Don't just concentrate on the object, concentrate on the person. Kiss them all over while you're doing it and talk to them. Get erotic, the whole ten yards.

What's the best way to get a skater to go home with you?
Lie on top of them and start humping them.

Well, that's direct.
[*Laughs.*] Just say, "Hey, let's go skating together." And then they'll want to hang out with you forever.

Ryan, 24

What's the ideal ratio for group sex and why?
I would think a threesome would be awkward because someone would get left out. I think you need a foursome.

A male in his late twenties hasn't had much sexual experience. He's nervous about it. Should he tell his new partner up front?
Yeah! He could parlay that into some crazy sex if he plays his cards right. If she's into that, maybe she wants to be the teacher. But you should be honest anyway because you can't lie about how much experience you've had. She's gonna know. "Whoops, wrong hole!"

Are there any words that should never be used to refer to genitalia?
I think "prick" has to go.

What's a pickup line that's actually worked for you?
"Your place or mine?"

That worked?
There was a lot of rum involved.

Sex Advice From

SLAM POETS

Dennis, a.k.a. MAD (Many Attitudes of Dennis), 32

Flow is obviously very important in poetry. Do you prefer a specific rhythm when you're having sex?

I'd have to say haiku. You know, three lines, seventeen syllables. Flow.

Can you give me some tips for talking dirty?

Well, for the uninitiated, you need to know how to say it without saying it, if that makes any sense. So you say something like "I'm gonna fornicate the manure out of your donkey." You've said it without saying it, and she gets the message.

So you don't want to start off too intensely?

No. You don't want to because women like the dirty talk, but they don't want to know that they're being talked dirty to. So you say stuff like "I can't wait to get some of that mmm mmm mmm v-a-gina." You see, that's how you do it. Flub it. Flip it. Tweak it a little. Tweakin', that's what it's all about.

What's a sex move guaranteed to make somebody scream?

I call it "come hither." A lot of men struggle with this whole G-spot thing; it's like the holy grail. I guess it's no coincidence that grail starts with g—the grail spot. You stick it in, reach up a little, curl the finger, do the "come hither" motion—come, come, come, and then come.

Advocate of Wordz, 24

🎤 Sex in public—are you a fan?

Yes, a big fan. The possibility of getting caught and going against what's against quote unquote correct. I love it. "Oh wait, we're in Central Park." "Oh wait, no one's around." I love it!

🎤 Any other places that are appealing?

Truth be told, I lost my virginity on the 1 train, going up to the Bronx. We were a litle drunk and, hey, it just happened. It was two or three in the morning and my girlfriend at the time and I were coming back from a party. I mean, what's as smooth as that Tom Cruise scene in *Risky Business*? [*Laughs.*]

🎤 What's a word that you should never use to refer to genitalia?

For a guy, "little." Don't say that, even if it is. For a female, "disgusting." You could scar their sexual life forever.

🎤 Slam poets have a reputation of being really intense and humorless. Is that true of you in bed?

Yes. Very, very true. Not much humor during the sex, very intense during the sex. Animalistic or slow and methodical. Afterwards, humor lightens every situation. So there might be a lot of pre-foreplay humor, and then afterward maybe some humor.

🎤 But during, you're focused?

Yeah. Basically, I'm in the zone. There's nothing funny about the zone.

How do you convince a girl to let you go through the back door?

It's all about eating the choche. You gotta eat the ass, massage the anus, work a little finger in there. You have to make sure she's relaxed, in a comfortable environment. It's something that needs to be talked about. Show your interest but don't force it.

What's a sexual mistake you want to warn people against?

If it's your first time with a woman, never do it if you're really drunk. That first impression is huge. If you're really drunk, your mind is elsewhere, your body's somewhere else. Then she's going to sit there, "That's how he has sex? That's awful." Make sure you're sober and prepared for that first impression.

Is there a specific move that's guaranteed to make somebody scream?

This is a really good one: while the girl is riding you, slowly stick your finger up her anus so your finger is stimulating her G-spot from behind. There's three different kinds of orgasms: there's the clit orgasm, the G-spot orgasm, and the both. That time, you're getting both. Even if one doesn't work, the other will, and they love it. And it can't be too hard, but it can't be too soft. It has to be the right amount. There's a science to it!

Sex Advice From

SNOWBOARDERS

Christian, 32

What's the best article of winter clothing to keep on when you're in bed with someone?

A pair of long fleece underwear. They're kind of snuggly, almost like pajamas.

Ever had sex in the snow? How do you do it without freezing to death?

Snow is actually pretty insulating. It can keep you warm, depending on the climate you're in. As long as the air is warm enough, you can just lay down in the snow on top of a jacket.

Have you learned any moves to use in bed from being out in the snow? Is there an especially athletic position you'd like to share with us?

In general being in good shape, having a strong core helps you fuck longer. It's all about the core muscles, the same muscles you use for snowboarding. That's why snowboarders make better lovers.

Jeff, 40

What's the best article of winter clothing to keep on when you're in bed with someone?
I would say a turtleneck. It'll keep you warm, but if it's form fitting, it can be really sexy.

Ever had sex in the snow? How do you do it without freezing to death?
I don't have much experience with sex in the snow. But if you want to keep your clothes on, I like the "Ballroom Dance." It's a kind of tandem technique for boarding. The man and the woman are facing each other, so one leads with the goofy foot (the left foot) and one leads with the right. And you go down the mountain with arms stretched out, holding each other close to the shoulders. It's beautiful to watch and you could say it's a kind of foreplay.

Tips for chatting up someone in a double chair without seeming creepy or making them feel trapped?
If you start a conversation about technique, you might be able to teach each other moves in the snow, which could definitely lead to other things.

Are hand jobs underrated? Tips?

They can be great if you have the right lotion. Hemp oils are always good, or try coconut butter.

The most unjustly neglected male or female body part?

I would say the ears. They're great for whispering and nibbling.

What nonmedical entity works as well as Viagra?

Try Rootsman Jamaican Vintage Roots. It cleanses the body and purifies the blood.

What's one thing everyone should have in their sex drawer aside from condoms and lubricant?

More condoms and lubricant. And you can get this special lubricant that heats up when you use it. That might work well for sex in the snow.

Rima, 26

What are the best resorts for hooking up?

I'd say Whistler. It has the biggest night life, and it's in the middle of that village. Also Aspen and Park City. They get a bunch of those Hollywood types during Sundance and then it's just tail city. Those Hollywood guys are the kind of guys who are fun to look at and have a drink with but you definitely don't want to go there.

The most unjustly neglected male or female body part?

For both men and women, it's the part on your ass where your cheek meets the back of your hamstring.

Is dirty instant messaging cheating? What about Webcamming?

No, it's not cheating. Males especially are very visual. I think they need a little bit of spice, a little bit of being naughty. I totally condone dirty magazines and videos. I think they're great, because that way a guy's having his fun and being naughty but he's not really cheating. I don't care how hot you are, it's hard to keep your boyfriend interested all the time. It's pretty harmless if it doesn't go too far.

What nonmedical entity works as well as Viagra?

Just good old-fashioned exercise. If you work out, you get fired up, you feel good about yourself, you have those endorphins running, that adrenaline. That's the best thing ever.

How can I give a woman an orgasm through cunnilingus? After I do, what's the best way to make sure she has another one?

Use your fingers while you're giving her head, one, two, and three in separate combinations. Lots of variety is best. Ask her what she likes. Listen to her moans and groans, have her communicate to you what's going on and try to match it, keep pace with her. And when it's all done and she has had an orgasm, it's time to fuck. But remember to ask her what she likes.

What erotic passage can I read someone to turn them on?

Instead of reading something written by someone else, read them something you've thought up yourself. That would be way more real and turn me on much more. I think I would just laugh if someone tried to read something from a book to me.

What's one thing everyone should have in their sex drawer aside from condoms and lubricant?

Really hot G-string underwear, and a very cute matching bra to go with it.

Jeff, 38

How can you have sex in the snow without freezing to death?

The trick is finding a tree your partner can stand against. Or you can put down jackets and lie down on top of them. In terms of gear, the hardest part is for the girl, because she has to be able to spread her legs, so you have to take at least one boot off so she can get her leg out. Otherwise, your only option is from behind. Location is important too. Make sure you're "off piste."

What about sex in a gondola? A chair lift?

Gondolas are pretty easy, but the problem is they're a lot faster than they used to be, eight minutes. In other countries you get a little more time, which is nice. At places like Mammoth they're windows all around, so you have to be a serious exhibitionist to get away with that one. I've been able to do oral on a chair lift. It's not as dangerous as you might think. It's hard to fall out because the chairs are tilted back. So you can sit on the edge. In other countries they have metal bars in the middle, so it's a little more difficult.

What are the best resorts for hooking up?

Las Lenas in Argentina is the very best. Unbelievable—the most beautiful women in the world. It's south of the equator, so you can go there during our summertime. And there's a great ratio of men to women.

I'm a woman in a long-term relationship. My boyfriend has stopped performing oral sex. I'm afraid to find out why. I think he's tired of me. What can I do to get him to resume?

Shave it. And bluntly tell your boyfriend, "Eat my pussy!" If he says no, there's definitely a problem.

Tips for recreational Viagra use?

I've tried the herbal Viagra. At health food stores, they have these supplements that have yohimbe bark, all this other stuff. That herbal male potency stuff, it actually works. I made the mistake of using it when I was with a girl I really liked for the first time, so the bar was set. She thought, "This guy was going to be like a porn star every time." Who could live up to that? On the other hand, I don't think it's important for the guy to be rock hard every time. Same for a woman: she doesn't have to get really wet every time. You don't want to put that kind of pressure on yourself.

What erotic passage can I read someone to turn them on?

Early Anne Rice. She used to write soft-core porn under a different name. Also the "Dear Penthouse" letters. Those were my favorite when I was little.

Sex Advice From

SORORITY GIRLS

Terri, 22

What are some sex and relationship tips that a "big [sister]" should always offer her "little [sister]"?
Don't date fraternity brothers! It's easy to meet fraternity brothers at events, but these same fraternity brothers meet every sorority sister in the country, and if this doesn't work out, then you'll still have to see them as a fellow Greek or when you go to a convention or a ball with your sorority. It's kind of like being on eBay. Everybody's bidding on the same people.

What's the most discreet way to spit after giving head?
Have something kind of there already. Most guys know you're going to do that anyway, so they keep a towel around or something.

What a gentleman.
Yeah. Just keep something nearby, and don't make a big show out of it. Don't make this ugly face, like "Oh my God." Just reach for the towel as if you're wiping your mouth at a restaurant, put it in the towel, push it aside, and then go about your business.

What's the best way to charm a fine sorority lady?
The key thing to remember is she is more than just her sorority. You shouldn't approach her just because she's a member of XYZ sorority—approach her for who she is. But to approach any lady, be yourself; you don't have to be super Fabio-romantic, Fabio-fine to approach her. Don't be intimidated. As long as you come on respectably, at the very least you'll get a smile and a polite hello.

Ellaine, 21

🐱 **I'm going abroad for three months. Are there any guide-lines I should follow for carrying on a relationship that I know will be temporary?**
Don't give your real name. Hey, you know it's temporary; you might as well have fun. Did you see that *90210* when Brenda went to Paris and pretended to be French?

🐱 **My boyfriend is freaky tall and I'm freaky not. Is there a sex position that would put us crotch to crotch but also face to face?**
I've never dated anyone freakishly tall, but I'd say sitting face to face, like sitting facing each other. That way he won't have to stare at the top of your head, unless he's that tall, in which case you're just shit out of luck.

🐱 **What's the best way to charm a fine Alpha Phi lady?**
Probably with some form of food. And yeah, a nice tight ass.

Laura, 20

🐢 My sorority sister gets slutty when she's drunk. Should I say something to her?

Yes, definitely say something to her. We have a rule in our sorority that no one wears their letters out to the bar, because even though they know who we are, it's not exactly the high ideal of womanhood to be walking around the bar being slutty and drunk. In our sorority you can get suspended for that.

🐢 What are some sex and relationship tips that a "big sister" [an older sorority member] should always offer her "little sister" [a younger member]?

Don't do it the first night. I am a big advocate for not doing it the first night you meet someone. Some people aren't.

🐢 The whole "it's college" excuse.

Yeah. I guess if you've known the person a long time it's not really the same thing . . . but fraternity guys aren't exactly, I don't know how to put this—aren't exactly the guys you want to go home with.

Sex Advice From

STAND-UP
COMEDIANS

Laurie, age withheld

🐾 Making a home video: do's and don'ts?

Hook your camcorder up to your big-screen TV and you can watch it while you're doing it. Know that you look worse than you think you do. You're really not that attractive. Your best option is to let your fantasies go and think you look hot. If you've seen how your ass works when you're getting it from behind, you'll never do it again.

🐾 How do you introduce toys into a new relationship?

Do it fast, and if they're freaked out by it, leave. They're not right for you if you like toys and they don't. You can be politically on opposite sides of the fence—I'm sure Mary Matalin and James Carville use the same toys. I say have sex early before you have any kind of emotional commitment. You find out if he's generous or if he's selfish while he's doing his best as a lover.

🐾 Tips for butt fingering during sex?

I've never gotten it, but I have given it and it startled the fuck out of the guy. When I feel like they're on autopilot, I slip it in, like, "Focus. Refocus, immediately." You want to sneak up. Kind of circle around, and then boom! Go in. It's like a spark plug or something. It's like plugging a guy in.

Robert, age withheld

When is it not a good idea to laugh in bed?

When a chick queefs. They get embarrassed. It'd be great if they laughed. That'd
be fantastic. It's just air coming out of her pussy. Laughing during sex, I mean,
if you know the person, it's cool. It can be relaxing. But if you don't know the
person, you better be Prince. Prince doesn't laugh.

Todd, 26

Finger in the ass during sex?
Oh, hell no, not in my ass!

For the girl?
Yeah. Just leave it in there and be like, "Heeeyyyyy! It's been in there for a while! Maybe I could get a second one in there!" That's the gateway to anal.

Are there any jokes that will guarantee you won't get laid?
Anything about fucking a dog will not get you laid.

STONERS

Jonathan, 21

Some argue that cannabis has health benefits, but does it have any sexual benefits?
That depends—if you smoke cannabis and then very soon afterwards have sex, then it's very much more enhanced, but that's only while you're at the sort of peak of the chemical alteration. If you wait a little while, your energy lowers and it's not good to have sex when your energy is real low like that.

Is the effect different for the different genders? I have female friends who say that when they smoke weed they get horny.
Honestly, I can only speak for myself, and sometimes it has an adverse effect. There's been times where I've meant to have sex and wanted to smoke weed to enhance it; but when I smoked weed, I ended up getting all philosophical and being like, "Why do I even want to have sex right now? Why do I do it? Why do I need pleasure?"

What's the best way to pick up a pot smoker at a rally?
It depends on your motives because there might not be a "best" involved if you just wanted to use that person. But if you see someone who you just feel a very intuitive, strong connection to—then I would say just talk to them. Be yourself. And depending on how strongly you feel, say it straight up, "I feel very strongly toward you right now." Usually that kind of honesty can be very effective.

Erica, 21

🐱 **Some argue that cannabis has health benefits, but does it have any sexual benefits?**
Well, in my own experience, when I smoke "haze," I get horny. That's about it, but besides that I don't think there's any sexual effect.

🐱 **I've heard girls say they get horny from smoking weed, but not guys.**
No, I've never heard of guys getting horny, I've heard of girls getting horny. My friend she tells me all the time that when she smokes she just wants to have sex all the time.

🐱 **In the name of public service, what's a sexual mistake you've made that you want to warn people against?**
That would probably be having sex in public.

🐱 **And why did it turn out to be a mistake?**
Well, okay, it was me and my ex-boyfriend and we were out on his deck, and one thing led to another, we started having sex on the deck and his next door neighbor came out and caught us. So that was pretty bad.

How long is too long to go without sex if you're in a relationship?

For me, personally, I can't go without it for like three days. I would say three days—that's the cutoff point.

If you're not in a relationship?

I would say two or three months.

What's the best way to pick someone up at pot rally?

Ask them if they smoke.

Well, here the answer is probably yes.

[*Laughs.*] Yeah, it is.

SUSHI CHEFS

Ricardo, 31

🍣 What do the following sushi orders say about a person's sexual tendencies/characteristics:

• A man who only orders California rolls?
He's the kind of guy who shaves his chest—and looks at himself in the mirror while he does it.

• A man who only orders spicy rolls and dragon rolls?
He likes rough sex and would be playful. He's really into trying new things.

• A woman who only orders roe, tobiko, and quail eggs?
She only likes missionary. It's hard to convince her to relax and express herself. She's self-conscious.

🍣 My sex drive has fallen lately. Do you have any suggestions for supplements or enhancers to rev it up again?
Seafood. I'm originally from Chile, and the seafood there is so good it even works for hangovers. In the morning, you should have seafood and lemon. Oysters. Fuck, those are good. Or have a seafood soup with mussels, clams, shrimps, scallops, onion, garlic. Natural stuff leads to natural horniness.

🍣 How does a person get a sushi chef to come home with them?
Good timing. The right look. And maybe just asking.

Max, 26

My boyfriend has no idea what to do when he's going down on me. How can I optimize his performance?
A girl I dated in college had a favorite trick she taught me. We were out in a bar one night, and she had a drink with a cherry in it. She asked me to tie the stem in a knot with my tongue, but I couldn't do it. She made me practice until I could. Then, one time when I was going down on her, she told me to do the "cherry-tying motion" around her clit. It was the specific movement that got her off, and she found a good analogy for it.

What makes for an optimal blow job?
The underside of the tip is an especially sensitive spot. When a girl rubs it with her tongue while going down on me, it feels incredible. But don't do it too hard or pinch it.

So what should I get at the sushi bar if I'm looking for an aphrodisiac?
I'm friends with a couple who hate uni and sea urchin, but they come in and eat it anyway, tons of it. They say they go home and have incredible sex. I'm more of a texture person, especially salmon, which has a silky texture reminiscent of labia. And don't drink too much. Sushi doesn't mix too well with alcohol.

I've been seeing a new woman. We've slept together quite a few times, but she's not getting off. How should I broach the subject? What's to be done?

I dated a girl once who took Paxil, so it was really hard for her to get off. Certain drugs designed to keep you normal can have some unpleasant side effects. Ask her directly why she's not getting off. Also, not all women scream. So talk about it. Once you open up a dialogue, it's easier to find better ways.

How should you tell your lover if their hygiene needs improving?

You should tell them outright. Or make suggestions, like to try a new soap. One of my old roommates got a gift of Kiehl's products, but he wasn't into bathing, so he wouldn't use it. But then his girlfriend took a shower with him and gave him a hand job with the soap. He said it was the best one he'd ever had, and now he only uses Kiehl's.

Satsko, 45

What sushi-making skills can you bring into the bedroom and use to enhance your sex life?
Dexterity.

What do the following sushi orders say about a person's sexual tendencies/characteristics:

• A man who only orders California rolls?
Boring!

• A man who only orders spicy rolls and dragon rolls?
He has great potential as a lover.

• A woman who only orders roe, tobiko, and quail eggs?
This would be a Freudian slip. She wants to have a baby—time is ticking!

What's the most common mistake men/women make during sex?
Overenthusiasm. Tell him to ease up and take it slow.

My sex drive has fallen lately. Do you have any suggestions for supplements or enhancers to rev it up again?
Lay off carbohydrates. Carbohydrates lower sex drive; protein revs you up.

Sydne, 32

What sushi-making skills can you bring into the bedroom and use to enhance your sex life?
Gentle hands, precise movements, and perseverance. The ability to go for a long time without stopping, without a bathroom break. And to scream at the right moments. When you're a sushi chef, you're screaming all day.

What makes for an optimal blow job?
Pretend it's a $26 order of blue fin toro. Be gentle and savor it.

What do the following sushi orders say about a person's sexual tendencies/characteristics:

• A man who only orders California rolls?
He likes fake breasts. California Rolls are fake sushi, it's not real crab, it's imitation.

• A man who only orders spicy rolls and dragon rolls?
He likes the Spanish ladies—he likes it hot.

• A woman who only orders roe, tobiko, and quail eggs?
She could be a lesbian. Or really into her own sexuality. Or probably she wants to get pregnant.

How does a person get a sushi chef to come home with them?
Sake, sake, and more sake. But whatever happens, don't insult their food. Sushi chefs can be so moody. You say one wrong thing, and you might not even know you did it. They just won't speak to you again.

TATTOO ARTISTS

Agent, 28

Sexiest location for a tattoo?
On a girl, the chest. A full chest piece.

The tattoo location and design that's the biggest turnoff?
For females, definitely shoulders and arms unless they're full sleeves. The single little tattoo sucks.

Do's and don'ts of a hand job?
Do use lubrication. Don't bitch when it makes a mess.

If someone gives you a rim job, do you return the favor?
Of course.

How do you give the best head?
I was taught by a lesbian when I was seventeen.

What did the lesson entail?
Technique, form, speed, decreasing speed, increasing speed.

What do you never say after sex?
"Your sister was better."

What do you always say after sex?
"Ladies and gentlemen, little Elvis has left the building."

Melanie, 19

Sexiest location for a tattoo?

For a guy, a real nice chest piece. My boyfriend has his penis tattooed, and I think that's pretty hot. It's like three stars right across the top. He showed me like five minutes after I met him, and I was like, "Hello! What's your name again?" I think the chest piece is also really great on a girl, like right above her tits. And the calves. Or right below the ass, on her thighs.

Tattoo location and design that's the biggest turnoff?

Tribal armbands. Worst thing ever. Tribal anything anywhere.

Do's and don'ts of a hand job?

Don't use your left hand if you're right-handed. Ask for help if you need it. Use both hands, sit facing the person, and use a lot of lubrication. It's the best.

Blow job etiquette: should a guy ask before coming in somebody's mouth?

No, because all that asking-questions shit ruins the mood. If you're giving a blow job and you're going to be highly offended if this person shoots a load in your mouth, you should tell them beforehand. Just say, "Let me know when you're going to shoot." Otherwise, don't fucking ask.

Most underrated erogenous zones?

Behind the knees and the belly button.

When sex starts to go bad in a relationship, how do you get things back on track?

Bring a friend.

Steven, 21

A client wants her honey's name tattooed across her ass. Do you feel obligated to tell them that their relationship is now officially doomed?
I usually try to talk people out of getting other people's names—boyfriend or girlfriend types—tattooed on their body.

How many people cover it up afterward?
A good 50 percent. I do a lot of cover-ups.

Tattoo placement and design that's the biggest turnoff?
I think tribal tattoos pretty much anywhere on the body are just awful.

Do's and don'ts of a hand job?
I don't even know where to begin. I would tell them don't forget about the orphans, you know what I mean?

Rim jobs: sometimes, never, or always?
Oh, man, to tell you the truth I'll lick everything.

Top five most underrated erogenous zones?
I think the hip bones, the back of the neck, collar bones are hot, and girls with nice hands are pretty hot. I've seen some girls with serious man hands and that's not very hot.

How do you get participants for group sex?
I hear going to Jersey usually helps.

Sex Advice From

TOUR GUIDES

Kenny, 39

Where is one surefire place you can go in any city and find sex?
In the red-light district. Every city has one, even if it's not obvious. Or on a tour bus.

If you're single, how do you pick up someone sitting next to you on the plane?
Touch them a little. Grab their thigh.

What sexual traits/characteristics could you surmise from the following:

• A male tourist who wears a fanny pack?
Actually, I wear a fanny pack; it's a place to stash my condoms.

• A female tourist who carries around a GPS system?
Obviously somebody who wants to know where she is at all times and where she's going, whether she's on a tour or in the bedroom.

• A woman who pulls out a huge map on the subway?
Obviously wants attention. She wants to make a connection.

Is pretending to be lost a good way to pick up a local?
I guess it could work, but it's not very creative. You really should come up with something better.

What's the best method of fingering someone?
Skip that altogether and use your tongue.

Norman, 43

Where is one surefire place you can go in any city and find sex?

The back of the alt-weekly newspaper. Of course it's probably part of an international sex slavery thing.

If you're single, how do you pick up someone sitting next to you on the plane?

On a short flight, begin with gentle queries. On a long flight, establish your help-fulness in passing things to the flight attendant and getting up so the other person can go to the bathroom. Or so they taught us in Tour Guide School.

What sexual traits/characteristics could you surmise from the following:

• A female tourist who carries around a GPS system?
A bit of a take-charge type, though that could invert in the sexual realm.

• A male tourist who wears sweatpants in restaurants?
May prefer beer to sex.

• A woman who pulls out a huge map on the subway?
Not good at sneaking around.

What happens on vacation stays on vacation: agree or disagree?

If it was accomplished while crossing the international date line, it never actually happened.

Mike, 32

Where is one surefire place you can go in any city and find sex?
Strip clubs. You know what you're going to get.

If you're traveling on a plane with a honey, what's the best way to make out with him or her?
Go to the bathroom when it's not very crowded. Go during the movie or when dinner has just been served. But it's just so small in there, I don't know how people do it. It would be better to get your blanket and cover yourself while you're still in your seat.

If you could have sex at any tourist site in the world, where would it be and why?
Of all the places I've been I would say Prague because of the buildings, the romance, the food. There are some sites that used to be old castles. You can find a lot of corners that you can slip into unnoticed.

What sexual traits/characteristics could you surmise from the following:

• A male tourist who wears a fanny pack?
Kind of boring, not original.

• A female tourist who carries around a GPS system?
She lacks intelligence. She doesn't like to take risks. Don't even try with her.

• A male tourist who wears sweatpants in restaurants?
He has no class and doesn't know what is appropriate. If you see this in Europe, you know it's an American. With a fanny pack.

Penny, 29

🐱 **Where is one surefire place you can go in any city and find sex?**
Sex may always be found in alleys.

🐱 **If you're single, how do you pick up someone sitting next to you on the plane?**
For women this is easy, just act a little afraid. Suddenly grab your neighbor's knee during take off. Then smile a little, apologize. From here you should be able to strike up a conversation. When turbulence hits, get nervous, grab their hand. Just before you land, thank them for the help, "It was my first flight, you were wonderful. Could I repay you with a drink at my hotel bar?" That should do it.

🐱 **If you're traveling with a honey on a plane or bus, what's the best way to make out with him or her without getting caught?**
When on a plane or bus, I'd say get the armrest out of the way, if possible. Then cover yourselves with a blanket or coat. Now get close as you can. Rest your head on your lover's shoulder. From here you can tease away the miles while others assume you are both fast asleep.

🐱 **Which chain restaurant is sexier: Applebee's or T.G.I. Friday's?**
T.G.I. Friday's.

If you could have sex at any tourist site in the world, where would it be?

Angkor Wat. A lost city in a steamy jungle is just sexy. Me Jane, you Tarzan!

What preparations do you need to make for great anal sex?

Time, tenderness, Tanqueray. Don't forget your lubrication.

What are some additional things to do when you're going down on a girl besides clitoral stimulation?

While pleasuring your lady orally, remember you were born with many tools, use as many as you can. The ones that buzz are especially fun.

If you had an itinerary for sex, what would be the first three items on it?

Slow deep kisses, curious hands, and three hours of free time.

What happens on vacation stays on vacation: agree or disagree?

Agree, unless it's good enough to bring home.

TRIBUTE BANDS

Mike, 36, Slippery When Wet (Bon Jovi tribute band)

What's the best song that you cover to have sex to?
"I'll Be There for You." It's basically a romantic song. It always works.

I want to role-play in bed. Would a rock-star scenario be good?
Based on fan reaction, I would think so.

What does every man and woman want in bed?
I would have to say oral sex.

In your experience what's the most common mistake men or women make in bed?
Probably lack of oral sex.

If someone wanted to pick up a member of your band, what would be your specific advice to them?
Look hot, and don't be too aggressive.

How can someone be assertive but not aggressive?
Subtle hints, a little bit of allure without actual touching.

And that's sexier?
I would say that's sexier. Too aggressive—ack!—you know? Girls think that if a guy grabs a girl's ass it's bad, but if it's the other way around, if a girl grabs a guy's ass, it's okay. I've had girls grab me and I've been like, "Whoa, why is it okay just to reach up and grab me?"

Joe, 45 – guitar, and Ray, 28 – drums, 2U (U2 tribute band)

What's the best song that you cover to have sex to?

Ray: "All I Want Is You."

Joe: "Where the Streets Have No Name." I like it a lot faster and harder.

Do you have sex to your version of the song, or their version?

Joe: Well, their version is ours. We do exact versions of U2 songs. If I could borrow Bono's penis, I would.

What are some tips for a one-night stand that will leave both parties feeling good about things?

Joe: The first thing is a damn good, expensive breakfast. The second thing is perhaps a room in the Park Meridian, instead of the Comack Motor Inn.

My significant other and I agreed to be honest about everything. Should I tell her about my wild sexual past?

Ray: No. Leave it in the past.

Joe: Absolutely tell. Some girls like hearing about your past.

Ray: And a lot of them don't.

Joe: Well, put it this way: the girl I would want in the present would want to hear about it.

Brian, a.k.a. "Diamond Dave," Eruption (Van Halen tribute band)

What's the best song that you cover to have sex to?
"Mean Street," off the *Fair Warning* album.

Do your groupies ask you to stay in character?
I can only speak for myself, but yeah. It's funny. They love getting it on with their favorite band.

My significant other and I have made a promise to be completely honest with each other. Should I tell her about my wild sexual past?
Yes, it'll give her something to shoot for.

I'm obsessed with someone who shot me down. I think we're perfect for each other. How can I tell if someone's truly uninterested or just playing hard to get?
Do what I call a "purse check." You get out of the car, and she's holding her purse in one hand. Grab her hand and see what happens. If she moves that purse over to the other hand, she's interested. If she doesn't, let her go.

Period sex: Yes? No? Methodology?
If it's with my significant other, definitely. If it's with anyone else, no. You don't need to do it that bad.

How can someone get a person in a tribute band to go home with them?
You've got to be one of the flashers.

Brooke, vocals **Lisa**, bass
Steph, electric and acoustic guitar and theremin **Wendy**, drums
Lez Zeppelin (clockwise from top)

🐾 What's the best song that you cover to have sex to?

Steph: "Black Dog," without a doubt. The last time we played "Black Dog," it was actually at a sex party. Women jumped on tables, tore their clothes off slowly, and then poured beer on themselves. The song has that effect.

🐾 What characteristics do you attribute to fans who lust after lead singers?

Wendy: Mullets, mullets, and Bud Light.

Steph: Rat tails.

Brooke: Tapered jeans, high-top sneakers.

Steph: And generally most straight girls.

🐾 Do groupies ask you to stay in character?

Steph: A lot them think that even though we're girls, we're really them. My theory is this: all of those fourteen-year-old boys who loved Led Zeppelin, and really wanted to screw Led Zeppelin, can now do that openly.

🐾 What are some tips for having one-night stands that leave both parties feeling good about things?

Brooke: Always call and say, "I had a really good time." Tell him it's the biggest you've ever had. That'll always make him happy.

Steph: That's a good one: "I don't like you, but you're the biggest I've ever had." He'll feel perfectly fine about that.

I'm a woman whose boyfriend is bi. I believe in monogamy, and threesomes are out of the question. Is the relationship doomed?
[*Collectively*]: Yes.

How can you tell someone their junk tastes like junk?
Brooke: Ask them if they've been eating asparagus.

What's the best way to give a woman head?
Brooke: The best way to get it is to wear a miniskirt. Tips? "The Shocker."

Steph: It's a certain hand configuration.

Brooke: The Shocker is really key. [*Holds hands in three-prong-plug style.*] The Shocker!

How do I get my partner to talk more in bed?
Brooke: Ask him hot questions. And spank him until he answers.

How can a person get a member of a tribute band to go home with them?
Lisa: Help us take the gear back. Help Wendy carry her drums, she's a cheap date.

Steph: Promise them some bootlegs that have never been seen.

Sex Advice From

TWINS

Drew and Jason, 24

My girlfriend hates the taste of my come. Is there anything I can eat to make it better?

Drew: I've heard that vanilla ice cream can do wonders. Don't ask why, but it seems to have a good effect.

Jason: Just tell her that it doesn't last too long and that she can brush her teeth right after. I have no idea if there is anything you can eat. Maybe something sweet with sugar in it.

What's the best pickup line we haven't heard a thousand times already? What's the worst twin-pickup cliché you've ever heard?

Drew: Best line, "Are you from Tennessee? 'Cause you're the only Ten I See." The worst twin-pickup cliché line I've heard is "You guys are like a stick of gum; won't you double my pleasure and double my fun?"

Jason: Best line, "Is that a mirror in your pocket? . . . 'Cause I can sure see myself in your pants." Worst twin line, "I have always wanted to see the Eiffel tower. What do you say the three of us go back to my room and re-create it?" (One in front, one in back, for those of you that are thick-headed.)

What are some good sex toys for beginners?

Drew: The best is body dust. It comes in two flavors. It is absolutely amazing.

Jason: Edible panties and handcuffs are always great.

Garry and Larry, 26

My guy's number one sexual fantasy involves twins. Why do so many men have a thing for double vision?

Garry: Always double your pleasure.

Larry: So if one sucks you always have a stand-in.

I have a very overactive libido and my girlfriend can't keep up with me. What to do?

Garry: Either get a blowup doll, or buy some new videos.

Larry: Or cheat, like the rest of America.

What's the worst twin-pickup cliché you've ever heard?

Garry: "I'll take one of those; make it a double."

Larry: "God knew what he was doing when he made two of you."

What are some good sex toys for beginners?

Garry: Go to a porn shop, and pick out what you like.

Larry: Feathers. I had a thing for Big Bird when I was little.

Pamela and Paula, 29

🐚 **My guy's number one sexual fanasty involves twins. Why do so many men have a thing for double vision?**

Pamela: Because men have a harder time being monogamous, probably.

Paula: They also might be curious to see if twins are identical to the last detail.

🐚 **I'm seeing a girl who doesn't give blow jobs and I'm contemplating dumping her because of it. Is there anything I can do to convince her before I take drastic measures?**

Pamela: Take your time with her, and whatever you do, don't show her porn about that subject. It will turn her off even more.

Paula: Let her know it's important to you, but don't beg. If she won't give in, you should probably cut your losses and find a more compatible mate.

🐚 **What can I do to guarantee getting laid on a first date?**

Paula: Be genuine and out front, and whip up a romantic evening. Bare your soul and be willing to wine and dine.

Pamela: Really listen to the other person and give them your full attention.

🐚 **Please share some tips for going down on a woman.**

Pamela: Women are all so different. Ask your partner; she should be happy to tell you.

Paula: Whatever you do, don't be sloppy, and remember rhythm is not just for dancing.

Sex Advice From

UNEMPLOYED
PEOPLE

Jessica, 27

Did you get more sex when you were gainfully employed or now?

Well, I live in Williamsburg, and like half the people don't have jobs. So if you're just walking around during the day, it's so easy to get laid there. I guess it depends on what neighborhood you live in.

Are there sexual advantages to being unemployed?

I'm a big fan of telling someone "Hey, I don't have to get up in the morning."

What is the best way to tell someone I want to be dominated in bed?

I always say, "If I didn't get bruises, I didn't have fun." That usually gets the point across. Wait, if I end up seeing that on somebody else's T-shirt, I'm going to be really pissed off.

What's the worst way someone's attempted to pick you up?

That guy over there [_points_] just a few minutes ago! He all came up and was like, "So, tell me—who did your tattoos?" And then, of course, he wants to show me all of his tattoos. That's the most annoying, generic way to go about it. Oh, it's also sort of a dead end when guys ask me, "So, tell me—what do you do?" I'm like, "Uh, I don't do anything. I'm unemployed."

Alex, 34

Did you get more sex when you were gainfully employed or now?

This is going to have to be theoretical. I haven't had sex in the last six months. Come to think of it, most of the time I haven't been having sex, I also haven't been working. Maybe there's a correlation there.

What qualifies as cheating: flirting, kissing, fooling around, or full-on fucking?

As a rule of thumb, I'd say anything beyond flirting is cheating. There are some people that say that even flirting is cheating. And when you meet one of those people, you should make a note to never date them.

What's the oddest thing that someone's asked you to do in bed?

Probably to repeatedly get her off and she never reciprocated.

Are you talking about oral sex?

Yes.

How long did it go unreciprocated?

[*Sheepishly*] Six months. I guess you could say I was exploring the boundaries of her selfishness. You could say I never found them. Or, more diplomatically, the boundaries of my patience were found before the boundaries of her selfishness.

A sexual mistake you'll never make again and want to warn others against as a public service?

Don't trust the rhythm method. Enough said.

Jess, 22

Is it easier to get laid when you're unemployed?
I think it's probably more a question of quantity over quality. I'd say that it's probably easier to get laid more being unemployed. If you're working, you probably have less sex, but it's with better people.

When is it okay to break up with someone over the phone?
I'm the wrong person to ask about this. I don't really initiate or end relationships. They just sort of spring up out of nowhere, only to eventually crumble around me later. A breakup over the phone actually kind of sounds good to me. That way there's no standing in their doorway in the rain at 4 A.M., tears streaming down my cheeks, pompadour wilting to the side, yelling, "I can change! I can change!"

My boyfriend is a little shy about having sex while I've got my period. What should I do?
What's a period last? Three to seven days? That should give you plenty of time to find a new boyfriend! I've never even heard of a boy that was unwilling to do that.

What's the biggest mistake a man can make in bed?
Have too little hand-eye coordination. Clearly, there are guys that didn't play enough Nintendo when they were younger.

Is there a good way to tell someone you have a penis that is so large it might cause . . . logistical difficulties?
Wear really thin, tight pants. Personally, I'm like, "Hi, how are you? How's it going? My cock is huge." Then later, "Hey, where are you going? Why are you crying?"

Sex Advice From

USED CAR
DEALERS

Dan, 29

🍸 **What's the best music to listen to while driving around with a potential lover to get them and you in the mood?**
I'm a Teddy Pendergrass man.

🍸 **What car model has the most adjustable steering column, so I can move the wheel out of the way while getting head?**
Don't worry about the steering column. Adjustable seating is pretty standard these days. This isn't an issue. She should be able to slobber away in a Daewoo or BMW.

🍸 **What sexual characteristics do you associate with the following car buyers:**

• A middle-aged man looking for a red convertible?
Messy divorce.

• A single woman looking for a family-sized SUV?
The upside is that she's an easy commission and possibly just easy. The downside is she easily gets attached.

• A woman looking for a pickup truck?
Independent. You should get laid pretty regularly, but may have to put up with country music to do so.

Luke, 27

What's the best music to listen to while driving around with a potential lover to get them and you in the mood?
You could always go with Led Zeppelin's *IV* but I have personally never seen a woman get really hot while listening to "When the Levee Breaks" or "Black Dog." Isn't Sade or Al Green the old standard? Jack Johnson would be good too, very soothing and not overly obvious.

What make and model do you recommend for backseat action?
With all of the SUVs out there, I would have to suggest something like a Suburban or an Escalade. Something huge.

I've always wanted a girl to go down on me while I'm driving, but I've never known how to bring this up with anyone I've ever dated. Any suggestions?
Let the car do the talking for you! Drive something hot, something sexy. Might I suggest the 2005 Porsche Boxster? Or you could be totally obvious, reveal all of your sinister intentions, and drive a Hummer.

Where's the best place to "run out of gas" and fool around? Any tips for having sex in a car and not getting caught? Any precautions we should know about?

Ah, "running out of gas." It never gets old, does it? I would have to say to pick some place where it's dark and quiet, where your girl is a little bit scared, but not so much that she's panicking and calling the police to come save you. Someplace you can concentrate on the matter at hand. Precautions about not getting caught? Just go for it! If you get caught, it was worth it, right? If you're that worried about it, public car sex is probably just not for you.

What's the best way to remove love stains from my car's interior?

Resolve Carpet Cleaner or peanut butter. Or is that gum? Regardless, love stains will come out with Resolve.

Garrett, 24

What make and model do you recommend for backseat action?

I'd say a 1977 Lincoln Continental with the bench seat up front. I really prefer bench front seats that fold down, kind of giving you a pleasure pallet for you and your lady.

I've always wanted a girl to go down on me while I'm driving. What car model has the most adjustable steering column, so I can move the wheel out of the way while getting head?

Trucks usually, plus the height really puts women at ease so that nobody sees them. They're always worried about being seen.

Any tips for having sex in a car and not getting caught?

I prefer behind a bowling alley or in the parking lot of a funeral home. Nobody ever goes there.

What's the best way to remove love stains from my car's interior?

They're called seat covers, man. They even come in animal prints. Problem solved.

Mark, 32

What's the best music to listen to while driving around with a potential lover to get them and you in the mood?
Prince is always good. I don't know many ladies that don't like Prince. If she doesn't like Prince, you don't need her anyway.

What make and model do you recommend for backseat action?
It has to be a big American car. I know for sure a 1980 Chrysler New Yorker is a good pick.

Where's the best place to "run out of gas "and fool around? Any tips for having sex in a car and not getting caught? Any precautions we should know about?
Best advice for not getting caught is to have tinted windows. Otherwise, do as much as you can in the front seat. If you're in the backseat, you're sure to raise suspicions. Roadside stops are always good.

What's the best way to remove love stains from my car's interior?
Scotchgard the seat. Then any simple cleaner and a paper towel should be fine.

Sex Advice From

VEGANS

Hugh, 30

Is semen considered nonvegan?

I would say no. A big premise behind veganism is that animal products are obtained nonconsensually, but in the case of semen, hopefully it's consensual.

What should one eat to improve the taste of one's semen?

I would stay away from things that are very pungent, like garlic. Overall, like anything else, if you lead a healthy lifestyle and you eat a healthy diet then everything about your body will be healthy.

Do you use any vegan paraphernalia (tofu, vegetables) as sexual accessories?

Green grapes. It's sexy to feed them to each other, going from mouth to mouth, from cleavage to mouth, from pussy to mouth. It's yummy and erotic.

Pubic hair—trimmed or natural?

I prefer trimmed because I hate getting a hair in the back of my throat. It can stay there for like a week.

If you (or your lover) are allergic to latex, what do you do? Is lambskin off-limits?

Yes. Absolutely. Lambskin is off-limits. Polyurethane is the way to go. Trojan Ultras are good. The thing about polyurethane is that the nature of it is entirely different. Latex is an insulator whereas polyurethane transmits heat so it's a different feeling. They're much, much better!

Marie, 26

🐚 **Do you spit or swallow?**
Swallow.

🐚 **Is semen nonvegan? It's the by-product of a mammal.**
I don't classify it as nonvegan.

🐚 **What should one eat to improve the taste of one's semen?**
Strawberries are good.

🐚 **Do you have sex with carnivores?**
Yes, but they taste different. Honestly, my ex-boyfriend was a vegan and his semen was much sweeter than the carnivore I'm dating now. It's a completely different taste. As unbiased as I can be, just purely talking about sex . . . the vegan boy tastes better.

🐚 **Have you ever experienced female ejaculation? And if so, how?**
Yes. It seems to happen more as I get older. It happens about half the time for me. I've had guys go down on me and say, "You just totally soaked my face!" And I say, "That's a good thing. Take that as a compliment!" There's a tribe in Africa, I forget where it is, where you're not considered a woman until you "spray the wall."

🐚 **How should a person suggest group sex?**
First, you have to figure out if your partner is into it or not. If there's even a remote chance, then go for it. I would suggest watching some porn that has group sex. If they're averse to porn, then they're probably averse to group sex. You can learn a lot about a person by watching porn with them. Particularly midget porn.

Freedom, 30

What should one eat to improve the taste of one's semen?
I've heard about eating strawberries. I'm not sure about that, but I would imagine anything sweet would do the trick.

Do you have sex with carnivores?
Yeah, sure. In my experience, the only difference is in personality types, not whether they are a vegetarian or carnivore.

Do you use any vegan paraphernalia (tofu, vegetables) as sexual accessories?
I'm not a big fan of the whole food-in-bed thing. I've been involved in some cucumber play. And, of course, when I was younger, there was that whole whipped cream fantasy thing. But that's not vegan. Other than that, I've never had much food interaction. It gets messy.

Pubic hair—trimmed or natural?
I get a bit turned off by fully shaved. I have a three-year-old daughter so it makes me think of little girls. When it comes to sex, I don't really care, but when it comes to watching porn, I do care more because you want to be able to see what's happening.

How should a person suggest group sex?
Well, with my wife it doesn't really take much convincing, but for someone else I would recommend discussing it first, way before it happens, because it can create a sticky situation in the relationship. Nine out of ten times you'll know if your partner is up for it.

Index

fuck buddies, 50, 51, 84, 144, 234, 252

gay sex, 17, 89, 91, 117. *See also* same-sex interactions

group sex, 21, 22, 99, 253, 287, 316, 317

G-spot, 149, 150, 163, 253, 257

hand jobs, 19, 49, 50, 59, 61, 125, 143, 145, 190, 192, 252, 261, 285–87

home videos, 18, 35, 36, 39, 103, 123, 125, 134, 135, 137, 139, 209, 271

hooking up, 42, 46, 120, 128, 182, 193, 210, 233, 262, 264

hygiene, 32, 87, 109, 164, 281

impotence, 101, 103, 133

Kegel exercises, 147, 150, 166, 191

kissing, 32, 39, 45, 60, 135

lactation, 148

lesbianism, 17, 102, 114, 215. *See also* same-sex interactions

lubrication, 106, 141, 147, 148, 150, 167, 261

massage
    oils, 121, 134, 138
    tips, 137–39, 141

masturbation, 13, 129, 237, 239

mile-high club, 75, 291, 292

mistakes, common, 80, 81, 100, 115, 131, 132, 134, 157, 159–61, 182, 223, 241, 242, 257, 276, 282, 295, 306, 307

mood music, 13, 14, 26, 56, 114, 175, 176, 179, 215, 216, 219, 220, 295–98, 309, 310, 313

morning sex, 32, 157

movies, 14, 31, 32, 65, 203–7. *See also* home videos; porn

nipples, 61, 148

one-night stands, 33, 89, 91, 193, 211, 296, 298

oral sex. *See* blow jobs; cunnilingus

orgasms. *See also* ejaculation
    faking, 178, 179
    female, 113, 114, 163, 165, 241, 263, 281
    inducing, 138, 139, 155, 165, 176, 215, 216, 234, 241, 263

outdoor sex, 68, 69, 182

penises
    bent, 153
    size of, 72, 167, 307
    terms for, 251, 253, 256

period sex, 297, 307

phone sex, 223

pickup lines
    bad, 73, 96, 301, 302, 305
    good, 13, 29, 33, 43, 46, 75, 76, 88, 90, 119, 151, 153, 169, 199–201, 252, 253, 292, 301
    unusual, 67, 72

pity sex, 80

polyamory, 161

porn, 29, 35, 154, 199–201, 237, 238, 249. *See also* home videos

pregnancy, 148, 149

prostitution, 13

pubic hair, 25, 29, 118–21, 169, 224, 227, 315, 317

public sex, 31, 36–37, 72, 88–89, 91, 123, 131, 256, 276